Mary's Voice

The Witness of Her Speaking Hope

Robin (Rochel) Arne

Mary's Voice

The Witness of Her Speaking Hope

Advantage
BOOKS

Robin Rochel Arne

Library of Congress Catalog Number: APPLIED FOR	
Name:	Arne, Robin
Title:	*Mary's Voice: The Witness of Her Speaking Hope* Robin Rochel Arne Advantage Books, 2025
Identifiers:	ISBN Paperback: 9781597558563 ISBN eBook: 9781597558723
Subjects:	RELIGION: Christian Life Inspirational Religion Biblical Studies - General

First Printing: November 2025
25 26 27 28 29 30 31   10 9 8 7 6 5 4 3 2 1

Table of Contents

Robin (Rochel) Arne

Acknowledgements

The people I learn from offer me hope in many ways. I am tied to the family of God and His influence on me comes forth by their hands. Many inspired me to perform in the value of the King. I am thankful to every one of them for the hope they emit. The power of the Caregiver is what keeps me doing this gift of writing. It is His guiding sight leading me to a hope filled unity in Him. He is a claim effect to my writing in where I offer hope to others. The support of God cannot be matched by another. I am given inspiration and unity with care at the core of all I entertain. The love of the Father is abundant and true. In Him is the lead I aim to have. The value of Christ is my passion. He is my mainstay and support beam. God cares for my efforts are tied to Him in a personal way. We act as a unified guidance measure. The knowledge is Scripture tied, and I am fed during the process of laying claim to the Most High. I shall stay in the path of my Savior for He is ever good to me.

Robin (Rochel) Arne

Gift One

Christ Is My Savior

God is working in my heart. He called me to Him in a special way. I am not a holy person with no impurities for I am flesh and bone as all others of mankind are. My heart is given hope due to the love of God toward me. His delight is my wish. I am not the one to apply hope to others by bearing the future Lord. It is God's role not mine. I can apply the training I have been gifted, and I can offer it to my child. I shall achieve the measure of faith and walk in the way of hope. I am not the way to eternal gain. That is the King's reward. How will I learn if not from on high? The lead of my hope is from God the Father. He is steady within me. I am merely one hoping to provide a better way for my child. I walk in the way of inspiration for God has spoken He is with me. I do not know all the trials which lay ahead, but the faith of my heart knows the saving way of God is good and righteous. To offer myself to the Waymaker is wise and unity is being had. I plan on the stand of inspired love for it is good to me to do this kind of thinking. At times I have fallen into a slump of fear for I am not all-knowing, and things are a challenge at times. But where my saving witness stands is with God. He is ever able to perfect my heart and make it courageous. I have the knowledge He is real, and I am standing firm He will aid me. I take to heart the plan of execution I am to display but this is the goal God will work through me. I have the work of God within me, and I am fed His support. Will I endure hardship or loss while carrying the Christ child? I have no knowledge of this. What matters is I continue to operate with character, and I look to God for the aid of my desire. God is the way to claim hope. He is the way of unity to the mind and the breath of Him is tied to me. I am not without the way before my mind for God leads me with accuracy. I offer what I learn and in the manner of sharing the light others hear what I know. The glory of the Waymaker is for all to know His good favor.

[18] This is how the birth of Jesus Christ came about: His mother Mary was pledged to be married to Joseph, but before they came together, she was found to be with child through the Holy Spirit. Matthew 1:18 NIV

The lead of my father is good and true. He captured me to Him in faith, and I gained eternal witness making. I have true knowledge for He gifts me His person in prayer and time vested toward His heart. He never fails in my mind, but I do have doubts for I am human. I believe with my whole heart, yet I discover I lose my way on occasion. Man's heart is a liar at times. I do know not to place my goal in the hands of myself for I cannot see into others. I look at what the Word of God states and I leave the details to the One of hope. God is my support measure and in Him I shall flourish. I am secure He knows my faith is genuine and orchestrates my unity in the manner of applying my dreams and goals to Him. Did I know I would carry this precious love for man? I stepped forward to God in the asking of Him. What will my daily assignments look like? I do not have the knowledge to do this. I am a mere woman with hope granted to her from the majestic Light, God Himself. I work where He leads, and I align to Him with care. How the many who hear of the Lord's work in me act will be their own identity. Leading is a plan of His and I follow Him with recognized insight. I have the necessary goals of being a good, providing witness to my child of hope. Will He stand as He should without my gain to Him with character as His birthright? Should I not say to Him His Father is the great I AM? It would be a lie if I didn't, yet many do not unite to this true word of hope. I would be skeptical too had the voice of the angel not spoken with true honor to the Most High.

[28] The angel went to her and said, "Greetings, you who are highly favored! The Lord is with you." [29] Mary was greatly troubled at his words and wondered what kind of greeting this might be. [30] But the angel said to her, "Do not be afraid, Mary, you have found favor with God. [31] You will be with child and give birth to a son, and you are to give him the name Jesus. [32] He will be great and will be called the Son of the Most High. The Lord God will give him the throne of his father David, [33] and he will reign over the house of Jacob forever; his kingdom will never end." [34] "How will this be," Mary asked the angel, "since I

am a virgin?" [35] *The angel answered, "The Holy Spirit will come on you, and the power of the Most Hight will overshadow you. So, the holy one to be born will be called the Son of God.* [36] *Even Elizabeth your relative is going to have a child in her old age, and she who was said to be barren is in her sixth month.* [37] *For nothing is impossible with God."* [38] *I am the Lord's servant," Mary answered. "May it be to me as you have said." Then the angel left her. Luke 1:28-38 NIV*

God is the way to thrive and have support. He is not without merit for He never fails. He knows the plan before it happens and, in this way, He creates the work of our hearts and minds to align to Him with favor. I know Him in a personal manner. It happens when I invite Him to gift me His heart. I pray and read Scripture to gain the support of our unity. I am the gown, and He is the whiteness of it. Being tied to the Creator is a gift I enjoy having. The goal of God is for His people to claim Him as their own. To know the saving way of true hope is to believe in the King of creation. The all-knowing One I have faith poured into. I am not the gateway, nor will I ever be the formal plan of salvation. I am merely the voice of a kindhearted person who embraced the Lord when He came to her. I did no special action because it was He who planned this idea. I now carry the wealth of man within me. Will this prove to be too difficult for me? God knows better than I do what I am capable of sharing to others. My unity to His spirit is what matters most. I am shielded by His person in the way of favor, and I will believe He is at work to gift me support.

My knowledge is for the man who places his mirror of hope to another. My years of growing insight have been few, yet I am here speaking on behalf of the Lord for He ordained me to stand on His behalf. Where is this to lead? Will I know the timing of His arrival? Will pain be present as it is with many women? God made me His child bride, and I am secure in Him. Where is the unity if not placed in His care? Sharing the light comes from on high. I lead where I am led to do this action. God supported me with care and unity. I see Him with clear vision. I invite Him to abide within me and in doing so I am given the faith I need to continue to align to Him. The shield of favor is mine in the way of support in the heart. God has never failed me nor will He for He is goodness always. The reward of sharing my knowledge is vital to the community I reside in. Will people come forth and believe me or will they think I am lying about my pregnancy? I did not expect to be given such a gift and I will not shame myself over it. I know God spoke into my heart and registered the goal so man can be invited to hear Him in a personal manner. Are the men going to stone me before the birth of my child? I do not believe this is how God will bring to life His saving power for how would the child then be offering salvation? I hear them speak of my fallen attire, yet I do not esteem it valued. God is my reason for sharing the truth of the union He presented. If faith carries the dream forward, I shall deem it as righteousness. The hope I know is all-encompassed in where the support needed to persuade men to follow the witness I profess is in the hands of the Creator. Leading is not my gift, yet, here I am carrying the Christ child. Support is the stand I see and know. God is my Father and in Him is the salutation He is favoring. Scripture leads me to the will of God, and I follow Him with character. He is ever before my heart, and I am glad He works in me. To know the One who made me His own is a sight of hope I have been given. I know my life has a purpose and I shall offer my insight to many. God is glorified in the way He made mankind and in the manner of Him we are united.

God is the one who made me His own and I am here to testify He is good and right. In Him is the knowledge man is His achievement. He calculated the reward and determined He desired to have a fellowship with mankind. He crafted each person to His liking and in the way of it man has favor. To know the One of hope is to claim Him as righteous. I believe I am here because of prayer from my forefathers who worked this area before my birth. The stand in the community came by way of faith and hope applied to the reason of inspiration. God, the all-knowing Being of insight, is my lead. He is all I hope to gain and here I am with His child within me. Should this be something, I fear? No, my Savior is coming to this region. Where is the reward if I cave and lose my hope? I would rather lose my own incentive than to adjoin in no unity to God. He is the gateway to life eternal. All the work of men cannot be gained until God ordains it to be. He is the great Maker of hope and leading. In Him is the sign of judgement and garnering of a witness for man to learn by. I am not the only one to know Him for He is the same to all men. If you serve God with love and honor, He will care for your heart and grant you recognized favor. The value of God is far greater than that of a small inherit stand of no character for He is better than all things known of value. My Creator is my signature of faith. He leads me into the brightness of His chamber when I receive Him with a witness of hope. To know God is to believe in Him with support. The way of God is for all to claim Him in a just way. He never loses to another goal for He is all-encompassing. He creates with golden, viable love so the work He does is true. I have the committed hope He will align to me for all time. We work as one and I am given the unity I thrive under. Leading is the hope I hear. The care of the One who claimed me is far greater than any other gift! Shielding the core of who I am is the One of might and true hope. I never have to fear I will fall into a minimal stand as God is my goalie, and He catches me wherever I go. I have the value of God tied to me in a personal way. It is significant and right bearing.

I am not the way to life eternal. I am merely the one God chose to deliver His child with merit. I liken my way of faith as that of all who place the value of Christ within them. Many have fallen into the longing of a Savior forgetting the way of the spiritual lead of God the Father. He is holy and true and in Him is our gift of unity. To know the One of hope is to claim Him with care. Leading is a stand God provides and in the manner of knowing Him in a personal way comes the belief He is good to the core. The way to gift another hope is to align to him with support. Sharing the plan of a witness in caregiving is what placed me within this role of leading. I chose to receive the Christ child, and I am holding Him in concern. The way it will come into play is not my understanding; yet I work as one who has the gift of sharing the light with those in need. God is my leader, and I know Him as good. He never loses His way with me, and I enter into agreement with His call. I realized God supports me no matter what takes shape around me. I love Him for the mighty gift He presents, and I honor Him with my intent. God is given over to value, and I long to serve Him with respect. He is committed to providing and my every need is understood. I share Him with those willing to hear about His great way. I believe I am no more than another for man is equal in God's eyes. The great true hope is the Child I carry. He is the way to life in abundance. I shall work to know my gift in a great unity for He is the saving measure all need to live with care and hope. I learn about the suturing, and I embrace the idea I am to offer comfort to the One who is within me. I shall not lose this knowledge, and I will gift it forward to those willing to gain from my understanding. The value of Christ is for all to claim, not one does He miss attending to. He can share His way forward and I am thankful He places me as one of His own. Together we tie in the unity and the support.

God, the way to life eternal, is the caring bridge of hope. In Him is the value of sharing light to many. I heard the sound of the spirit and in its call, there was unity given. I am not the mighty goal of man for I am made as he is, slight in form and build with no special powers. I place my heart in the hand of God knowing He is ever faithful to me. I share with others who created me in this way. I am the tying bridge He is using to gift mankind a pathway to Him. I shall never hold the value of the righteous God for he alone is the Creator of hope. I build in the way of knowing where I am to act and in doing the work of God man is being gifted life eternal. How this will happen is not for me to say. I am simply following my Lord into acting inspiring the faith. Leading so others find the unity is wise for us all. We should prepare any who need knowing the Living God called Father I Am. I bear witness to His holy way and in the manner of sharing this truth I reward the King with my dedication. To learn where to offer gain is to achieve the stand of insight provided in the Scripture material. Having the lead of a woman of character can be had by any who place God above all else. I am not a woman of no hope for God supports me in the way of favor. He made me a gift to mankind only in the form of bearing His child to give witness to the world. It shall be as He decides. I am not the wise insight. That is the Holy One's burden. My shoulders are slim and made from bone and flesh. This is proof I am not the Lord on high. I could never sew the plan God placed for me to work toward. I am not the way to life eternal; yet I am bonding to the One who is. My stomach protrudes so I am aware of the contents I carry. Another could have been chosen but I am the one who was ordained. In the way of sharing the gift I must support the lead of God to Him. He will need instructed care where He is taught the light of God and given a way to know

Him by witnessing His mother pray and worship the Living Word. I am not the one to implement any unity for that is God's spirit doing this. I merely believe and act in accordance with Him. The love of God is for any who share Him with the heart and mind. Within man is the ability to portray the light and grant it to others. Knowing the care of God is wise and good. In Him is the unity to build and operate with true wealth. The meaning of support is not how the pocketbook leans in the testament of desire but where the faith of man resides. That is the suture for the soul to bear witness to. Goals of light bring the plan of man's care forward. In the actions of reading Scripture man gains the righteous way to be. Shelter from God is a formula all need to survive.

The way to thrive is felt by the one who declares love to others in a spiritual way. The time of hope is built on true gain in where the heart is not a direct stain to mankind. It takes the beauty of God for man to learn where to plan and how to operate. I am not the way of favor for it is God who performs this role. In Him is the stand of support needed to carry forward the light and the unity. His way is favoring the one who believes in Him with support. I am not the instrument of hope for the Creator is this setting. I see man has favor when he places his heart toward the great I Am. The knowing place value to His person with support and insight being gifted. My righteous way is no different than another who knows his King and Lord. The baby in my womb will maintain man not I. A false account could be thought if one believes I am special and unique and not merely a female in human form. I have no gift of power different from mankind, but I do realize I have been granted the love of the One who made me. I now act with care so as not to harm this precious unity I hold dear. My support to man will be that of knowing the Gateway known as Jesus for that is the name I was given to claim my child's birthright. God is the Gateway to life eternal and in Him I have favor. The spirit is solid in me for I study the light of God through His intent in the Word. God is precious to me, and He never leaves me nor abandons my heart. I have belief in Him and He is the way for me to invest. I place my hope in the palm of His hand, and I am tied to His way of being. It came to me to act with a suture from on high. The battle of not believing is not for me. I stand in the knowing way of insight and with this measure I am fed unity. God ties me to Him, and I am thankful He does.

> [15] *Can a mother forget the baby at her breast and have no compassion on the child she has borne? Though she may forget, I will not forget you!* [16] *See I have engraved you on the palms of my hands; your walls are ever before me. Isaiah 49:15-16 NIV*

Fruit of the heart is favor in its finest glory to God. When a person decides to align to the Waymaker good intent is had. The value of strife is shallow so work to be the hope another finds as a solid goal in the way of presenting light and good faith. I am not the lead of inspiration for it is God alone who claims this as His own. I shared the birthing of insight due to reading the Scriptures I was taught. Knowing the One of pure light is a unity I embrace; yet I need to be tied to Him in a fast manner. The support from on high is never without love and guiding. I deliver this unity when I offer to others the value of God. I shall not accept another's viewpoint without God being the goal for me. I have the will to know where to offer love and in this way, I guide those less fortunate. The vocation of light comes into play where man is fed the hope of Christ. My child is going to be this to mankind. I do not know all the manner of Him for He is greater than I. However, I will work to gift others the care and support I have been given. To love the Waymaker as I do is significant and justified. Leading is for any who have the unity to God before their hearts. The work of sharing the knowledge comes where man invites the love of the Caretaker to himself. The invitation of God is for all who believe and accept Him as their Lord. I do not anticipate being called the One of pure love for that is God alone. He is the one I believe conquered death and made a plan for all mankind. When this is revealed, I will understand it better but for now I stand in the way of sharing this unity. I do not engage with doubt as it is not what preserves my heart. I place the unity of God to my heart, and I share this with any who ask what my knowledge is made from. God is the spiritual One of unity and in Him is the tying of a light beam to the heart of mankind.

Christ is my anchor, yet I have not met Him. He is bound to me through the Scriptures of hope. In the gift is the support needed to carry forward the reward man needs to blossom and thrive. I am given hope due to the reading of the Book of light. The reward far surpasses that of no insight. It leads me not to do harm but to offer inspiring gain. I value the work of the Jewish people and in the way of the commitment from the hand of the Savior I know freedom exists. No one who places his attendance on the church body is ever without guiding faith. I know the way to prosperity is found in the call from on high. He is the source of my gain. In Him is the sound of a guide who never fails. I have the idea of knowing where to offer another the gain I received. Learning and to carve into the way of faith is to offer it to others in need. The proper way to align to the One of hope is to give your heart to Him in free abandonment. I have the heart of the King, but I have not seen Him. I feel Him moving within me and I wait to hear Him speak. Will I know Him as the gateway for life eternal and will I believe in Him as the Holy Master of mankind? I look at myself and think how did this come to be? I am a simple person without wealth, and I am not given over to fame or recognition. My Lord determined me to have this blessed gift, so I aim to stand on His behalf with support. Knowing the way to life eternal is a stand I need to guide from. The value of a just gain is not one of no inherit trust. It must be a qualifier for love to be had. God is my support measure and in Him I know peace and good harmony. He is the way to life with purpose, so I plan to offer my heart to Him in a steady way. His unity to me is far above man's support. I know I am not missing Him for He is here; yet I am tied to the Father as one in saving power. I learn about the Savior from reading the Book of Hope and in its contents is the managed favor I need to flourish.

46 The LORD lives! Praise be to my Rock! Exalted be God my Savior! Psalm 19:46 NIV

Christ is the one who made me a caring individual. He did not fail to support me when I was small and learning His value. He taught my heart the way ahead and I am fed love by His manner of insight. The prayer field of favor supported me with caregiving. I learned how to carry out the faith and where to offer it toward others. The support was a boost to my person not just of self. It was the unity to Christ. I never felt small or insignificant, but I know I am valued with great hope. God is my benefactor in where I stay hope filled to Him with love. I shall receive the marked name of virgin until this birth of the Saving One happens. The child is not to be found lacking for I have been given truth to hold fast to. I know I am not a reactive person, and I work with care when talking to others. I guide them where able and I engage with support if hope is present in the conversation. If no fruit is offered, I do not entangle my heart with that person because there is no point to it. God is supportive to me, and He is the foundation I need to flourish. In the calm of the day, I wait for God to enter my thought process and lead me with character. God is righteous and true, and He places value on my faith. I accept He has a plan of hope for me to follow, and I offer my heart for Him to guide. In the way of sharing the knowing gain many are hearing of the child within me. He will align mankind to Him, and the door will be opened for man to have eternal witnessing for all time. Will it look like the Scriptures foretell? Yes, as the Word of the Great Influencer is always true! I shall have to endure the death of my God and in the way of it I will get a guide measuring for eternity. I am not one to cause harm to others, but it will not be an easy stand I must endure.

Leading is not something I claim forward for I speak where God gifts me to. Men are the ones who have the gift of sharing; yet God granted me the hope of Him through the male network. I am not given over to foolish comments about my growing child for I am secure in the fact He is from God above. It is difficult to always be joy filled when men attack my character but to serve the God of man is a unity I uphold. The movement of my baby speaks to the gain of Him within. I know I am fed with courage, and I act with this knowledge. I valued my Savior, and I look forward to the blessed event of His birth! Will I be afraid as all women are when bearing a child? I am not more than they are so I believe it will be as stated. God will support me through the offering and in the way of Him I will have comfort.

Jewish people are my heritage. In the way of hearing the Savior, they will know Him in a personal way. It will be from His hand they find prosperity. It will take good intent for this to happen. The one who knows the Lord is a saved being of hope. I am standing on the love of God due to His factoring my hold with Him. We are tied and in good standing. I view Him as solid and good. I never have to worry where He is moving, for, He guides my every step. I look to His favor to decide where I am to step. It will be as He decides for me to have His care provided. I know I am one of many who placed her heart in His control. The unity is gold to me. I call Him Lord in respect to Him. The unity we have will never fade as I intend to always work with structured maintenance. In the Word of Him is the fruit I need to hear the support and goal making. I shall not assume I am more valued than another for all mankind is God's idea. We have different roles to serve Him; yet we are one with Him, with Him with courage. He offers my heart the work of His person and I accept it with merriment. The lead of God is not of a simple hosting. In the way of Him is the unity man derives as just. The invitation to Him is a simplistic unity but one of merit and faith. The glory of His saving ability cannot be measured. In Him is the sight plan of favor far above anything else. God supports the work of His calling, and I stand at the ready to offer myself to Him. Does this mean an advancement in my station of life? I have no authority to this. God is supportive and good to me in a unique way, but I am not one of more wealth than any other with the support of care to God. In the way of faith, I am a singular being of inspired goal setting. I hear my Savior speak and I engage with hope. He is my all in all. I am not above His instruction nor am I greater than He. I am not His equal nor will I ever be for I am mere flesh and bone made from the dust of the earth.

> *[7] The LORD God formed the man from the dust of the ground and breathed into his nostrils the breath of life, and the man became a living being. Genesis 2:7 NIV*

God orchestrates the love of Him to His many followers. Though none may aim for the love of God I will stay committed to Him with care and hope. He has me in the palm of His hand, and I am given the unity I need to flourish. God is the mentor all of man needs to abide with growing in support to others. I learned my Savior is to come forth and I am to be His mother. I will rear Him with love, and I know He will stand as a right bearing sight to my person. If the value of Him is just and holy I will not be alone in the way I stand on His behalf. I do not doubt it will be but for me to unite to my own baby will be something of a faith stand not that of a witness of His knowledge. Once He grows and offers me the hope of Him, I will learn more than I can imagine at this time. He will feed my heart, and I shall not be without the unity of His counsel. Jesus will be His surname, but my own object of faith will offer to Him the Word of who His Father is. I shall claim it to Him to know the Word of the living God and be inspired to read the Scriptures and gain the knowledge of Him. He shall need rearing as He will come forth as a baby from the womb and not a man of full adulthood. How this happened was a gift from the Holy Spirit. I did not do any action to bring this about. I am a virgin with no forthright gain from the act of mating. I have the birth to guarantee the stand of the Lord gained me a child but the way of it is a mystery. I am here as one of the many who placed the value of God within them. It is gold to my heart to be considered of value to be the mother of the Christ child. I am not special nor am I different from others who believe in the One of Hope. I simply invested in the Word of the Lord and He chose me due to it. I am not the way to know prosperity of the heart for that is God's unity not my own.

The value of the One who planned my birth is the same invested Caretaker who supported me with this blessed fruit I now carry within me. God supports the one willing to believe and stand on the value of His person. Christ is the gateway to learning hope He maintains within a person. A fellow believer has the knowing way of support necessary to thrive and gain in the way of true hope. One must offer the fruit of the Word to learn how to discern who the King is and how to know Him in a personal manner. Will there be a different viewpoint concerning how to align to Him? I am not the one who knows this answer. I too will have to see what comes from this offering I carry. I am here as a witness to the way of life and how it is happening within me. I simply know I am pregnant without having been gifted with a child in the usual way. I am tied to the Gateway by way of blood and flesh, yet I know I am not the same as He is. The aptitude of my child will be far greater than what I am able to stand on. I have the learning of a small child in comparison. I shall know who to share the Biblical way with when God shares to me who it should be but my stand on the promise of God remains in full effect. I am not the singular reason man gained a way forward. It is the love I carry within who holds this honor. I am given the knowledge, I too, am with care and I willingly share this forward. God is the way to eternal unity. It is by His witness I know I am fed support. Leading is not my gift. I offer what I gain but to know the One of hope is to realize the great God of all has put into action His love and favor. Knowing the way to instruct is for the many who place the value of God to others. All can emit the goal of faith by guiding those in need. I have the support of the Waymaker due to my own unity to His person. I invite the love of God to me in a caring way. I enter His presence in prayer, and I align to Him in character. How do I stand where no other has trodden? I know my Savior is good and true. He will lead me with support, so I do not travel alone.

My mighty, caring Lord is always working for the better of my heart. I am here due to His favor and in His value system I am fed truth. I look to the way of God to go and to be heard. I am not one to know all the way of Him, so I invest in reading the Word and grow in prayer to Him. The value of His caring way is far greater than all I have known. I am not in the way of no hope for God has shown me I am given support. He speaks to my heart, and I gain from Him in a spiritual way. To love the One who made me is wise and good. The Lord gifts me unity and I learn from the way He operates. Where a person finds faith is the swell of insight favoring the righteous. God is my mainframe and in Him I am given hope. He is hope bearing and true. He never leaves my side nor will He ever. I have Him close to me and He leads me with true gain. I know He is the way to prosper so I witness His good support and share it with those looking for a way to live in harmony with Him. I know He is all-encompassed so there is never a less than unity to Him. His call to my heart is a stand of growing hope. Every day I learn and develop a way to stand with character. Even though some do not believe how I gained a pregnancy I do not dwell on this negative thinking. Once the favor of birth comes to be people will know I speak the truth. I am not one to follow the way of deceptive thinking nor will I venture into it. The light from God is far better to my heart and mind. I am ever walking in unity to God, and it pleases me to act in such a way. The value of sharing the light of God is far above all else. I am giving others the choice of hearing how I came to be the gifted one to bear this child of hope. I say what came to me in angel form and I invite the willing to hear my profession. If accepting God means to have to endure a difficult time, I am willing to offer my abilities just the same. God is my measure of hope not mankind. I love the way of God! He is my all in all.

My own way of being is not the value man has to me but rather of God to my heart. His value far exceeds what man may have contrived. If ever there was one to love above all else, it is the Risen I Am. Will this happen in the way I envision? I do not know what it shall all entail for I am merely one of hope not all-knowing. The true Lord of man is the one of insight and gain in where man finds the value of God to his person. I am here due to God creating me not me making my own way. To learn to contain my excitement has been difficult due to the knowledge God granted me the Savior! He is the unity I love and in His value system I am fed support. God operates where I do not. I stand in recognized honor by some who fail to unite to the Waymaker. They look to me for insight I do not have. Value is the King alone not I or another. To share the work of God so others gain is all I can put forth. This is in the way of unity to God not to me. I stand on the life of God within me not my own merit for I sinned as all mankind does. I am not tied to the Waymaker in the way of no value for I am His child of faith. He worked in me a new way of being and I am grateful for it. To love my God and to follow Him with bounty is to record His way as my own inheritance. God supports my effort to stand on His behalf, but He does not need my aid. I am not the reason for life eternal, and I never will be. If I could take my part and add it to God's value, I still wouldn't be someone of hope. God alone is this measure. He ordained man to know Him in a personal way and this gift within me shall be the gateway for this to happen. I am here due to God's timing and in Him is the real idea of fruit to the heart. Capturing my soul came from His hand not mine. I would have perished had it not been for God's endearing ability to take me from the ash heap and apply His saving grace. I endure the ridicule as I know I am His bride. The one He determined could stand on behalf of the promise. I shall hear my child's voice and gain in the way of it but knowing Him is the true honor. He supports me and I witness His approval in the way of staying in a committed bounty and reward unity. He sees me as I am and still, He holds me fast to His person. The knowledge of God is for all who place their goals in the palm of His hand. He shall not offer Himself to those who stand off and refuse to claim Him as the Savior. God is the reason man exists. Without this truth man would have no hope of having life eternal in the way of support and goodness. The all-knowing God of man is the sole Being of inspired favor. He does not separate Himself from those who need Him for He cares for all both great and small in standing. Even the birth of my child will represent this truth. It will bear witness to the goal He is above man in all He offers. He is righteous and holy with caregiving so deep and vast man cannot compare.

I am not tied to the One of inspiration for the factor of knowing freedom alone. I have faith in Him and He is my captured audience. When I gift Him time and honor He supports me in the way of insight. I am glued to His way of being and the will of Him is heard. I have the witness of favor due to the gain I receive from above. The unity is far more than I am bound to understand but I do witness His glory feeding my heart. The value of His person is for my own support to be had. In the way of unity, I am tied for all time. How did this come to be but for Him alone and His care for me. I feed those who come my way, but I am not a measure of hope. God serves me the stand, and I claim it as my way ahead. I look toward the King, and I embrace Him even more. To learn from Scripture the unity and guiding necessary to align to God is good for the spirit. The unity I am gaining is far greater than I imagined it would be. I truly embrace my God, and I invite Him into me with hope. The lead of the One who preserved my heart when the call came for me to offer myself to Him in such a way as being the mother to the Creator is my discipline. I shall align with care and support my baby with the reward of being His disciple. In the manner of knowing where to step for the unity to be a grounded gift I am not all-knowing. It is a daily practice I gain from. The support of my guard is God above. I stand in honor of Him, and I tie to Him with respect. To learn the love of God is a goal I offer forward. In it is the unity I press to others. Sharing God is a gift and I value it greatly.

[1] *As a prisoner for the Lord, then, I urge you to live a life worthy of the calling you have received.* [2] *Be completely humble and gentle; be patient, bearing with one another in love.* [3] *Make every effort to keep the unity of the Spirit through the bond of peace. Ephesians 4:1-3 NIV*

My Lord is the one who made me the glue to the world in that I feed hope due to the love I share of God. The offering is not supernatural because I am mere dust of the earth. I have the hope I will bear witness to the value of God and be a person of true honor toward Him. I shall have to prepare for the birth as any other woman would do. I am not offered to man as one might think, for, I am the way of the measure not the unity of God but of His gift to me. I am tied to Christ as He is the one who performed on my behalf. The child I bear will resemble the likeness of my mind not my physical being. What will I call Him? It is stated in the truth I heard the angel speak His name. Jesus is the name of the hope of mankind. In the stand of sharing this knowledge I grow with the reward. Reading the fruit of God's Word has shown me how to love and to witness so others learn as I have. I am not the Lord's only choice for sharing the light. Many have this unity with Him, and I am given the knowledge due to the plan of Him being my aid and counselor. The work of God is far reaching and in the way of knowing where to offer the significant design element I gain recognition. I am tied to God with care not just value. He is the reason I exist. In Him is the plan of salvation and He used me as a partner for this to happen. Should I feel honored? Would it not have been another if I rejected the request, so I look to God for the glory to be had? He is the Creator not me, a singular being of His molding. The hope of man finds the work to be a growth where love is plentiful. If value to God is heard, a calm will be had. I know I am merely thinking on the way of a birth to come but I am sure I will love this growing claim with every breath I take. The Risen God of man is far more than a tiny baby within me. For the Spirit of God is abundant. He has always been and always will be.

My focus is the Savior not my own abilities. I am not the goal for that is God's lead, but I do value this enrolment, and I embrace the hope it provides. The value of God is for any who have the need to learn who He is and how He performs. Instructing the learned comes to the offering with clear intent. But man has fallen short of the glory of the Great I Am, so he needs to have a way to have unity with inspired gain. God's work is abundantly clear to any who understood the unity to Him. There has always been a plan of hope for man to follow. I know this child is the stand man needs to have a gateway for all time. God will not leave any in the dust when they pursue Him with abandonment. Leading is a mirage if man is the one doing the activity of it. But where the Lord enables good, harmony is had. The lead of the One who performs for man to inherit the love of God is He, the Almighty. The activity of God is to secure man to Him with prosperity. The veil is going to be removed, and man is going to have a better pathway to the Father. Why would I be a witness to this happening? God placed me in the seat of inspired gain simply for the sake of knowing freedom for those who value Christ. I am not special or unique as far as being superior to another. I am made of the same material all of mankind is. I have a gifted way of sharing hope due to the application of faith. This is the thing that called me to God. I knew He meant more than any other thing. The support from Him is far reaching. Any who admit God is the saving way to life eternal gain the hope He offers. The love value of God's care cannot be measured, nor can it be held in the pocketbook. To know God is to ascertain He is the source of favor not the rule of the day. He has the ten commandments to follow but man is incapable of meeting the stand, so he needed a way to have forgiveness present. Blood is the way for this to happen. Animals have been the means thus far but now there will be a new means for this to develop. I do not know the details or how this will transpire but I share the value of my child to any who call me blessed.

The Lord, my Helpmate, is the way to thrive with care. To know Him is a real gem of the spirit. I take my yearning and offer it to Him and He cares for me through the meaning of it. I am not the sincere Being of all for that is God Himself. He aligns me to Himself, and I stand on the love He offers my heart. I invest in the holy way He manages so I build with honor to many. The value of the One who made me is standing in the mirror of hope toward my heart. I'm a reflection of His person due to the study of knowing Him and seeing His counsel. I have the support of His mind in that I read Scripture, and I tie to it with insight. He claims me as His own, so I am not without the gift of unity He provides. Care is built where He upholds the individual who offers his desires to Him. The work of God is for man to find prosperity in His way. He ordains the heart to follow Him, and I have the inherited dream of knowing His stand. The way of God is sincere and true.

He leads me with support, so I do not fail. I look at where He offered Himself and I believe I am part of the work He gifts. Many have fallen prey to no knowledge for they have not engaged with hope toward His person. The Lord is holy and true. He will perfect the one who professes He is good. His name is Savior, and I know He is real and true. I have no doubt He stands with care toward all who call on Him in prayer. I work so others learn and have the knowing way of His support. To offer the dream of God is a secure formula to advance the heart into Him. I invite all to claim the Risen Way and I evaluate where He is to be found. The lead of my Lord is a good, impressed manner. I am not tied to the darkness of no hope for with God all things blossom and are committed to faith. To love the One who made you is for the heart to accept Him with support. I pray so I do not lose my connection to Him. He offers me a direct line to Him in this manner. Gain a way of hope by feeding your plan to His lead. He will teach you where to walk and how to gain recognition so you can further the way of His stand. The care of God supports anyone who places his time and talent in His hands. He is without harm to the righteous. Leading is for a man of purpose so place your intent toward a righteous way and guide the less knowing into the light. Bounty will be had, and truth will blossom.

One of hope is given to offering the light of Him so many can have an abundant way of life. The work of God is a draw where light and hope reside. The will of God is for man to know Him in a personal way. God supports the love He holds in the manner of faith to Him. He provides the lead of His intent so others can achieve and find value. Unity is far greater than the knowing hand of mankind. If you feel a tug within your spirit, you are being given to offer a willed conscious claim God is true. Honor it with support and invite the Savior into your person. Fear holds many, so fight against it and thrive with purpose. To follow the Waymaker is a plan of integrity. Show support by applying Scripture to your daily practice. It will provide unity, and the gateway of growth will enhance your heart. God illuminates the way for a better adhesive sight of knowing to evolve. He is faithful to the way of His being. His formula is solid, and it contains the spirit of Him. We have value to the offering if we support the way of it. To align to the One of insight is a plan of hope no one can compare to. I know from experience God is favoring to the righteous. I am not without sin, but I support God with my whole being. He is the plan of my life. I invite His counsel to me and in the manner of it I am fed insight. I gain in the way of knowledge and the plan for me is solid with favor. This birth to come will be no different than expected but the plan it represents shall shine the way for mankind to live in harmony with the Lord. I invite this process though I do not know how it will come to be. I am simply willing to serve my Father and support His goal for me. To gain in the way of a child is a gift saying greatness is being had. All families have gold where a child has been gifted. I know no other way to share the offering than to express hope is at the door.

The love I have for the One who made me His own is great and unfolding in such a way I always dream of Him. I am glued to His person and thank Him for the hope He is bestowing my way. I have the will of Him within me, and I aim to carry forward instructing this child so others can have hope too. Glory to the One who mastered my care field and supported me in the way of faith. In complete hope I found favor. It took no action of my own for this to come to be. I am here due to the value of God not my own merit. I am a person who supported the Lord. I am not His maker. To learn where to plan and how to offer others the role of partner is not for me but for the Creator. I am here as a witness the Lord lives! I am not the significant way to life eternal, nor will I ever be. Man found the light in the way God portrays it. I am not one of insight, but I learn from His counsel. Scripture feeds my heart, and I offer it to others. Where I am tied in care so is the unity I need to breathe in support. My womb is a holding plan for the Son of God to be given life. But I know had He desired a different formula to bring this birth into the mainframe of His person He could have chosen any path, and it would be so. I value my King and who He is to me. I shall not stay content until the plan of salvation is fulfilled. I know I am to adhere to the work of God and to ingest the offering with caregiving. A baby is a bright adhesion to God no matter the condition of its siring. Life is an abundance of inspiring unity. Some fear a birth as that of no hope, yet I see it for the sacred bounty it is. Revealing the hope of man to himself is a gown of support vested with prosperity. If another had been chosen, would she have offered the same idea making or am I the one of true honor for this role? I do not know the answer to this as I am not the one to deliver hope to mankind. All the people in the region are learning of my trial. Some proclaim me a liar while others believe the truth of what I shared. I must not reject this beautiful dream, and I need to honor my Lord with support. Though I am small in comparison to another I have the goal of sharing my gain to those willing to learn from it. I invite the role of life giver, and I adhere to the offered support by way of knowing I am fed unity through it. The insight I have is from on high. I know I am here due to the great King being with me through this challenge. I have the unity in respect to the sight of the Word and due to its support, I am stable and smitten with care. The lead I offer is not for any who have the desire to harm me or this life I carry. I shall not invest where I am not welcome to do so. I tear away the fabric of false leading and I offer the light of the saving power to all who believe. I am not a teacher but one who knows Scripture, so I recite what God declared. In the manner of it I gain too, and many are fed inspiring truth.

[4] Show me your ways, O LORD, teach me your paths; [5] guide me in your truth and teach me, for you are God my Savior, and my hope is in you all day long. Psalm 25:4-5 NIV

Gift Two

My Child is the Waymaker for Mankind

My honor is the same as it would be for any who God would have chosen for this gain. The Spiritual lead of God is for man to learn and gain insight, so he has a pathway of support. God is never one to perform for the sake of no hope or fortitude. In leading man is given the reward of sharing the sight of God to others who share the value of Him. I have hope within due to the reading of the Book of gain. In the manner of it I am given support for training this child I claim as my own. God supported me with care and in the making of this emblem I am spared the loss of no insight. To care for another is to align to God and to declare Him righteous. I have the value of the One who made me, and in the unity, I am given true honor. The learning time was a Godsend, so I know I am with support and direct contact has been gifted. I look to where the unity came from, and I know it was sent from Christ Himself. His leading gave me the order of His counsel, so I have the growing heart He witnesses to. The work of my own hand is not complete till I commit to the way of true hope. God alone is the one who offers such great return values. He is the standard I claim as good. I am walking in favor due to the honorary lead of His heart to mine. I am not without fault for I am flesh not all spiritual. I failed in many areas of my life, but all mankind has. I am not set apart due to having a better viewpoint nor am I given over to a length of hope no one can compare to. I merely invite the Word of God into me, and I let Him gift my knowledge forward. The way of giving life to a baby is the same for me as it is for any woman of the human species. I do not enter to this lightly because I am tied to the care of this birthing, and I know there will be pain and loss of blood just as there is with all childbearing. The lead of God to me will not be of no ability to offer a plan of hope. My invested manner is tied to the way of eternal gifted planning not my own merit. I learn as man does with the content of Scripture being applied to my way of living. I am here as a support beam not the gift to man but the holder of Him. Currently, I yearn for man to align himself to God. There has been through time the objective for man to do so. It is man's own loss not to stand with care toward Christ. The lead of Him is of righteous gifting so man has the hope of a life in good company not of death with no purpose. The reward of knowing the Great One of hope is a sight all need to be given in favor. I shall always contribute my hope to the One who made me.

The reward of knowing the way to work for man is from the Creator not me. I bear witness to the way of God for I am not the reason for life eternal. To pray to one who is not God is false, and I will not practice such falsehood. I lead with care, and I work like any other for the value of my Savior is far reaching. I am tied in the unity to God's care, but it serves all man in the same manner. All of man is with care whether he admits this truth or whether he denies it the offered hope is present. To work with correct measuring we are taught in the Book of reading and in this unity I remain. I learn to conquer my doubts about where a lie comes into play. I practice the Word in my daily life, and I invite the hope of God to me. I aim to be standing in the light, and I am intimate with God due to reading the love of Him and by speaking to Him in prayer. My daily practice is to discern who is registering with me and who is false to my heart. I reject any voice of dark enterprises which releases me to offer hope in their place. I value the commitment of God to me, so I enact the same presence to Him. He is the way to thrive and in doing this unity we tie together with care and support. God is the suture to man necessary to bring about a good, invested goal. The Lord Himself is our mainframe. He is the unity belt I wear. To know God and to align to Him with care is to shower Him with our being. We are weak in comparison, but God has chosen us to align to Him just the same. He values our hearts and minds in such a way all we are can be significant to His way of being. The right thought process of knowing where to offer insight is a plan of hope He provides. His care is far more than a simple gesture of intimacy. In the correlation we have investment of eternal hope. I know man is never going to see God completely for He is far above our understanding; yet, to know Him is a gift in and of itself. The shared bounty comes to the one who places value to the King. Our goal of knowing where to gift others value is from the God who made us righteous. Through the love of Him we are tied to the goal of sharing intimate details of His character. God is perfect and true. Man is weak and frail; yet, in Christ man is given hope.

God's care supports all who have the will to flourish and give others the fruit of God to many. The value of the one who professes to prosper due to the saving witness God provides means to align to His care with unity. God lights the way for others to know Him and to hear His speaking to their hearts and minds. It encourages the support of God to the way of His care. I have the heart of Christ within me, and I offer it to the people willing to gain from the example. I value the work of God and in Him is the fruit of His being. To know the way to educate others comes from the application of reading the Book of Truth. I know I am ever with courage based on the unity God provides. He teaches me the hope and in His way of presence I am fed clarity. God performs so man is fed favor. To know the One of great hope is to be seen by Him in support to another. I believe I am tied to the way of speaking and the hope it provides is clearly my offered stand. I have the inspiring hope to gift another the unity I share from on high. The work of my spirit leads me to secure the value of God in perfect example. God is the factor I am tied with. The swift unity man needs can be had with a simple profession of hope to God. It is the measure of unity providing the favor that supports us with insight. The value of faith is to align with care and structure. God performs so man can have the plan of eternal unity. I am here as an example of hope due to the heart of Christ, my miracle worker. He is ever my faith partner, and I am given in hope due to His performing within my heart. The shoulder work is not that of no bearing. God is perfect with a true way about Him. He never loses His step or has no perception of what needs to be. I have the support of a mighty caretaker! He teaches me where to go so I do not lose my way. I am sheltered in the gift of His perception to my own upright care due to Him.

Many have the support needed to find prosperity due to trust in the One of intent. The favor of God far surpasses that of a lone individual of man's making. A meaningful expression of the Gateway is coming and in the mixture of God to Him we are to be united in care. I have the unity to this knowledge due the realization God performed on my behalf. I value this gift, and I work so many can have the gift I contain. I shall not hinder the work my Lord is doing. I will offer the true hope I have been supporting. To learn where I am to offer growth is a stand I engage forward. God is all-knowing but I am not He. I do not have all the answers for man and his required learning. I am merely one who takes the name of God and places it to her with care. I shelter my heart in the palm of God, and I look to Him for the placement of my entire support. He is the Gateway I need to gain freedom in the spirit realm. I direct many to the plan of the witness I now remain with. It came by way of support from an angel of mercy. He spoke true to my spirit that I would offer my physical self for carrying this treasure. Did I know I would have this reward? I never envisioned I would enable man to know the Savior as I am. I work for unity not self. I lead so others find the plan of the witness I hold. In the way of sharing the offered hope I find the role of support needed to offer another the respect of God and who He is as my inherit life change. The lead of God supports any who claim Him for their own way. I stand in the shadow knowing I am not the only vested person who claimed God as Savior. I evaluate where to offer my knowledge and I lean into God with pure hope. I invite His leading so I can exist in harmony to Him. In the way of sharing His gift to me I shall acclaim Him as good. The bread of life is God not me. I am not the one to declare sins toward for I have no ability to offer freedom from them. The blood of the One who will be crucified is the main focal point for this to be understood. Do I ever dream of how it will impact my life? I would not be human if I did not.

God is true to His nature. He never changes or loses His persona. In Him is the light of growing care. He is value and marksmanship supporting His cherished people. He will not run from the battle of hope. He supports the people who claim Him as their own. In the forthright group of knowing agents who serve Him in a free manner faith has been granted. I know God is all-encompassed, yet He yearns for my honor to be His. I am standing on the provision He made so mankind has the benefit of my labor. To know the speech of the Savior is to read the Book of moral righteousness. Scripture is complete to the heart and mind. It never fails nor does it lose its value. To

Gift Two: My Child is the Waymaker for Mankind

read the light is to offer your heart and mind the gift of it for all time. It is not forgotten even when one walks away from the bond of it. God is the plan for man and in His Book is the birth of knowledge. The darkness must flee when it is applied to the heart. If you have lost the incentive to align to Christ know it is due to your own admission, He is not your whole point for existing. You turned from Him in some form or another. Man, often denies the power of the saving way. God supports the work of any who shared the Gospel and made it victorious to their person. Unity is a draw and in it is the calm of the heart. Some believe if God does not gift them the gateway to hope in an immediate response, He has not fulfilled His offered way. This is false. Hope is built on the faith of a person and his intent to God. It takes a partnership for love to blossom. If you enact a low value to the Risen Waymaker you receive a false idea that leans to the negative. It will permeate your heart and mind, and total loss will climb. To learn to fight against this falsehood is to stand in the way of choosing the light over the tempting dark idea of no real maturity to the mind. God is the gift man needs to blossom and in the way of His call comes the ability to keep the growth of the Word. In the stand is the balcony of leading where one is applying himself to the hope of God. It is a claim of support necessary to thrive. The perfect way of sharing the Bible is a solid investment no other can compare. Voices of people in the way of insight are not wise choices if they pursued something other than the righteous truth. It can only be acknowledged if God is the support value. To love the care of God but not adhere to Him is a loss from the start.

> [13] *But we ought always to thank God for you, brothers loved by the Lord. Because from the beginning God chose you to be saved through the sanctifying work of the Spirit and through belief in the truth.* [14] *He called you to this through our gospel, that you might share in the glory of our Lord Jesus Christ.* [15] *So then, brothers, stand firm and hold to the teachings we passed on to you, whether by word of mouth or by letter. 2 Thessalonians 2:13-15 NIV*

Grow with care and fire the intent toward the work of God to many. He hears the offering and supports the value of His counsel. I act as a voice of support due to my training in caregiving. It has come by way of knowing the light from on high. I offer the aspect of sharing light, so others find the prosperity I know. It is not a simple gesture of no intertwining love for God cares deeply for my person. He is not divided in the way He operates. Any who have the value of Him find favor from His hand. He is the way to prosperity and to know His call is a plentiful way to act. I have the work of a mother before me. Shall I invest in another form of commitment when this is what I was called to do? No, for I value what my Savior is connecting me to be. I have the support of His garnering and in the value of Him I am given faith of insight. No voice of doubt will claim me where God sanctioned me to thrive. I am not the way to ever after for that is the lead of Christ, but I know I will follow Him just the same. He is ever within me due to my acceptance of Him. Both His body and His spirit reside in my flesh but once I deliver this Child, I will have the work of sharing the gospel to Him. How this all develops I do not know but God has shown me the value of this unity. I know the intent is for me to share the birth with many and to offer the growth of God to those seeking Him. Shall it happen directly on meeting Him or will it take time for Him to build character? I do not believe He will lack any teaching of hope for He is the Gateway for man to know God the Father. They are one in unity but separate as well. It is deep knowledge to invite this truth to the heart; yet I stand with the favor of it. I know many who accepted this as the way of insight, and they too understand God is at work. I will respond to the One who asks of me to learn His delivery of Scripture. I will engage where He commits me, and I shall offer what I witnessed. To know I carry the Christ Child is a grant of hope I claim as true. Knowing God is a plan of acting I adhere to. I shall align to this knowledge and be standing with care for I am to deliver the birth with hope and committed faith.

God is committed to sharing His honor with the one who places Him first in his life. The offered way of His care comes to the man who witnesses hope and puts it in motion. God is reflective to the man who places his heart in His path of opportunity. Teaching is for the one who learns and believes in the great way of faith. Doors open when man prays and listens for hope to be given. A lead may be different than one first realizes. It may be of a sincere outreach with no strings of dark gathering in its circle. Value is found in the plan of the Almighty. He is ever with courage to mankind. I am here for the way of His counsel to be given. I do not hold the answer to life eternal nor am I to be prayed to. I simply know God and who He is to me. I work so another can have the plan of hope, and I endear myself to Christ. He is not in this world, yet, in flesh and blood, but He does exist in my womb being formed into a Being of inspiration as a witness of hope in flesh form. He already is living on this earth in spirit form. How can man differ from one to another if he does not truly know the Creator? He will offer no value if He abstains from the hope of God and He inflict loss to His caregiving. I know I am tied to the way of God for I believe in the truth of who He is and how He manages. The value I have within is far more precious than the lead of my need to be standing with no purpose. I act with care, and I lean into the One who gave me hope. I am tied to Him due to the value of His caregiving. He made my heart enjoy His love and it supports my daily walk.

My unity to the One of hope is for man to see and embrace due to the offering it presents. In the way of care God is more valued than a precious crown of gold. To know the One of insight is to claim Him as the rightful lead to man. I know man is tied to Him when He places the value of God on the forefront of his faith. The reason I declare God is good is due to His caregiving to me. Each person I know decides whether he will continue in God or step outside of Him. I accept this fact, but the better way is to recognize God with support. Believing is what stands in the manner of hope. Not all who say they know God truly do. It is the one who places his idea making in the palm of God's hand who realizes the hope He carries to him. The value of God is far greater than the reward of no hope which is given from the stand of no fruit. God's light is greater than the greatest star. He is the way to thrive and have abundant living. I am gifted the Child of glory due to declaring God is real. I stayed in faith and offered it to many. Did I know God would call me to be His choice for carrying the Christ Child? No, I did not know in advance, nor did I think I would be given such honor. The value of God is far greater than I can imagine but to stay connected to Him is my dream for all time. Leading comes by way of insight. It is processed where the mind and the heart embrace the offered truth. God is the Being of inspiration. In Him is the unity I desire to achieve. The hope of God is with me in a personal way. He teaches me to stand and to support others. I endure my way of knowing Him to many. I lead where I am able, but I know God is the real reward. He is the gift all need to achieve in a bountiful manner. Suspect is my own inclination at times for I am one of man not that of being the King. I preserve my heart with the need of God, and I recognize I am weak. If a faulty way of thinking comes into play, I aim to remove it quickly. The gain is hard and I once more stand upright. Satan attaches to the one who places value to what he states. He is mere death nothing more.

To listen to the believer and hear his testimony is a sound way to know something transpired within. The unity of Christ is far greater than the mission of knowing another human being. God is the one who plans the spiritual lead and in Him is the following of insight one needs to transform into a being of light. Growth occurs where the might of God is forecast. I have the will to believe and to plan so another can gain from my offering. Leadership is solid and it means to apply the heart to the growing care of Christ. If no unity is tied no root has been established. Why is due to the individual not truly believing God is who He claims to be. It takes the knowing heart to evaluate the light and to spend the time needed to witness this role of leading. The membership gains in harmony where one is fed the fruit needed to flourish. Stand in the care of God and deliver the hope to others and the gateway of leading will be plentiful. It may be you are given the light for the reason of knowing who to witness toward and how to worship God in the process. The need is everywhere as man is not all-knowing. He needs to hear the love God offers and read of the hope He provides. God is not one to align to the way of another for He alone is the all-knowing Being of insight. In Him is the gift of the perfect sacrifice. I do not know what all this shall become and how it will perform but I know God does not lose His stand in confusion. The lead of the Caregiver is a solid intent man is given. The total of a heart is not the message if it does not value the role of God's unity. I am here working to share the plan as I have the gift within me. I am not the way forward, but I do strive to be a member of the bride. The people group who will align to the will of God and be a witness to His performing way. Have there been others who led as I am? In all the Book of the Hebrew people records show this to be the case. I am stricken with hope and not of loss in training how to align to God. He has care and support for the man who places his draw on Him. To know how to gift man the hope he possessed is how one to another can act.

I have the belief I am not the only person who has the work of God within him. The people willing to boast about God are the waymakers of hope God provides. Learning from leading their hearts is a beam of instruction showing moral righteousness and good manners.

My support is from the One who made me His lighted plan. I grow each day in size, yet I do not feel overdrawn to claim I am the gateway to all. I have the knowing aptitude God created this life. I am not the way of it, but I shall teach what I know to Him. He shall hear the light, and it will develop within. I grow eager to meet Him face-to-face as every mother whoever carried a child does. I yearn to know Him intimately but in truth I already do. I am tied to Him with support for He has always existed. There is no measure of time where He was not here. I know I am talking to the man who prepares to witness as I do. I have the unity to know who He is and how He works. I gift man the will to learn by sharing my daily life. It is a good platform to operate from. The work of God in me is the whole point to my life. In the suturing of His name to my person I have the work of His caregiving within me. Both my body and my spirit embrace the light. I am complete in the manner of knowledge because I endeavor to read the Book of Hope. It is for my counsel in the truth it feeds me with pure goal making. I do not forestall the wait by applying more incentive for God has already carried this burden. I enter the gateway of favor for this is the will of my heart. I am different in that I know where I came from. God formed me in the womb and grew me to womanhood. The support has always been a part of me. I did not achieve it on my own merit. I invited the Word of God to my heart, and I fed from it. The way of knowing the light and what it holds for me is a divine knowledge I hold fast to. The growing care I offer is due to the love value God has given me. The worth of Christ is far greater than I will ever be. No man can claim he is better than the Living God of all. The example I carry is the fruit of the Caregiver not my own self. I shall forever be grateful to God for sharing this gift and I will plan to align to Him in faith. For this is the growing way of Him to me.

My baby is the Child of light. In Him man will learn to live in a rich way. He shall not conquer with fear but with love and good hope. To know His person will be a measure of fruit no one can compare with. How do I know I am chosen to carry this birth? God showed me with an angel of insight. It was a considered way of pure favor. I did not expect it, nor did I prepare to be the mother of the King. I learned God manages in His own way and He leads when He chooses to do so. What happens is a sight plan of good hope not one of no-good harmony. God prepared many to learn and offer His moral code. I am one such person. I do know I need training in Scripture because it is the value I know makes me stand in insight. Comparing myself to that of God is false. I am merely a person of human flesh where God is spiritual. He claims to be righteous, and I am only in the way of knowing Him and keeping as He directs. To witness the value of God is what happens to me when I stand with courage to Him. I evaluate what is considered good and I know only God alone is righteous to the core of Him. I am one who believes in the Savior, and I engage with hope due to His deliverance to me. Do I at times think I am one to save another? No, for I am not capable of this feat. Only God above can do this act. I am faulty as all of man is. I do prepare to be enlightened to offer others the fruit of God to man. Should I be a judge of him? No, but I am given the way of God, so I see where man fails. I look at what matters to the Lord, and I invite His way to my heart. I am a shelter to the Word, and I stand on its reward. The Lord is not weak nor is He without a manner of pure wealth. Meaning He is more than a trophy to mankind. In Him is the work of a great leader. None can offer the same stand for only God is the viewpoint of goodness. In Him is a solid grooming and always has been. He had no need to gain knowledge for He is complete. How can this be? Only God Himself knows the answer. I do not expect to have all the knowledge He does as I am not a King as He is. I enact the Word, and I enter in harmony to Him. He feeds me the plan of a witness I learn by. Knowing the Word is what fixes to me how to keep. I shoulder no other, but I do witness to some who offer a lead for me to do so. I am here sharing the light due to my own intent being of courage in faith. God supported me, and I want the world to know this. He is ever in my heart, and He will always be there. I plan to grow in reverence to Him so there is never a time where I am without His witness to me in a personal way. He stands in wait for me to always abide with love to Him. This means something to me. I look at His support and I gain in the way of it. Would I ever vanish from His viewing? No, for He is the One who mastered the mind and carried to me the goal of hope.

> *⁹ The LORD is a refuge for the oppressed, a stronghold in times of trouble. ¹⁰ Those who know your name will trust in you, for you, LORD, have never forsaken those who seek you. Psalm 9:9-10 NIV*

My caregiving does not match the One who made me but rather it enhances His instructed learning. The voice of reason is my Savior Himself not I. I gain in the way of every other man on earth. I am taught to learn and to invest in Christ. The goal for me is to deliver the Child of hope not to be His master. I am tied to His eternal way, and I thank Him for allowing me to cherish Him with support. I know man can perform so others can find support as I have. That is why I witness to the many who come to me for hope. I do, however, know it is the Savior who I am delivering. I have the knowledge due to the Word of God being spoken over me. An angel of light came to me and shared this truth. Did I receive the gift of the Child right then. I do not have the knowledge of how it transpired but I do know I am smitten with the work He performed. I value my God, and I believe in His support to me. I share the light and in Him is the unity I am to claim. Knowing where and when to all things is not something I am able to perform. I have the same makeup as all humans. God did not make me as He is in the way of His gifts and talents. I am light to man due to His way of being within me. I am ever hoping for advanced care from His heart. This is the unity I aim to gain for it far out ways the burden of my own existence. The goal of sharing the light is for all mankind who places his manner to that of Christ. He is ever the guiding instructor who ordains me. If you value the work of God and share Him with those in need you have gained Him as your support beam. I thank my God for delivering me from sin and for showing me the better way. He alone delivers the spirit to His mansion in the sky. I am without the work of Him only when I reject His support. I uphold this knowledge and supply it to my heart. The knowledge is made clear to me when I pray and read Scripture. The value of His counsel is glory to my heart. I shall never lose the foundation I have due to His support for my being. He alone is the gateway for man to thrive.

My perception of God is holy to Him. He is the One of inspiring gifts that support me. I let Him lead and I am fed the hope I need to flourish. My growing care to Him is ever building and I look to His support for my daily activities. I am broad and given to life-giving inspiration. This is what I measure my good intent on. If I lose interest in a goal, it is not from lack of clear thinking. It matters to the One who created me whether I offer the plan of unity, or I lead in my own stand. I captured the one willing to learn and approve of God's care. It is a simple thing to offer another light. Fear is not part of the witness measure. For some it is difficult for they have not timed their meet to God as righteous and true. It takes practicing the love of God forward and in the right way. Knowing the Word of the Lord is what determines whether one is visibly on trac or losing his path of hope. To tame the spirit is how I perform. It does not mean I stand at an angle or lose my way to Him. My voice is heard, and I enter His calling. My volume is rising as I am tied to Him more every day. To witness His good claim to me is an abundance I hold dear. I am ever grateful for Him. He ties to my heart, and I hear Him with clear unity. It is not a simple thing to have been given God as my focal point. It is the great way of faith found in support of His making. The power of His call is quiet and true. It does not boast or stand loud. It is revealed when one enters a commitment to the Great I AM. It is an offered lead no man can offer so, enrich it to your heart and know unity to God. I savor the light of knowing the care is found in God above. Through Him I am fed support and goal making develops. I am vested with caregiving and I know I have the unity desiring little other than the true One inspiring loyalty. The shared unity is for both He and I to enter an arrangement of faith. I value my Lord, and I work with His caregiving due to His way within me. Those who entrusted the Savior with their hearts are given the bounty of Him for all time. This is a present state anyone can receive. The simple profession of faith means the tie is complete and true hope is granted. My Lord will bring this calm to many and in His way of livelihood all will have the reward if they choose it. God is complete and holy never with a loss or negative. If you receive the gift of salvation you are chosen by Him with support. The acceptance comes from you, not His intent but your own. It acts on your part and once you determined the way of God is better than all else good unity will develop.

God is the means to knowing how to act and where to achieve. His value to mankind is simplistic and right. Due to the love He has for any person's willingness to know Him God can be granted the favor of him. The knowing will continue in His claim to them. It is a whisper of a voice, but it is mighty and true. The value of Christ is a claim to mankind He never fails nor will He. His manner is developed with the true work of His being. The plan to know where to find Him is nearby. The heart is pulled to Him when it is embracing the knowledge He offers. The value of God is far greater than of the average human being. Man is tied to the witness of Christ, but it is Him who feeds the spiritual being. Any who feel defeat need only invest in the Book of light to gain in the way of faith. But one must place value to it to be granted the witness it holds. The reward of man is to know the care and support God provides. The belief of Him is the equivalent of faith but it is the action into it that makes it cement. I read the Book of Learning, and I gain from it due to the belief God is speaking to me with it. Unity is far above my own understanding, but I gain just the same when I invest. Learning more aptitude is a sign I am in the manner of faith. I invite my God to witness to me, and I let Him divest to me where and how to perform. The negative fades away and growth begins to bloom. I draw on the manner of God and in Him I have the relished idea He is mighty. I know He is perfect in all He does. He plans my outlook, and I invite Him to dine with me for support.

God, the one of light, is for me the best influence of sharing the hope forward to many. I am tying my heart to the care of God knowing in Him I have value. The way to gift another support is to offer it to the one in need. I share due to the value of God and His caregiving is a witness stand of stamina. To align to the bead of the Great God of inspiration is to attract Him to your person. This comes by way of uniting to Him with concern and favor. Our own unity to God comes into play where man determines to rule with hope. The goal of God is far greater than all the work of the heart with no intent to learn who He is and how He works. God is all-powerful. He could simply maintain us and never speak forth to our honor but that is not who He is. He is faith bearing and true. In Him is the insight we need to endure in His call. I have the initiative to learn and invest in the way of God, so I am fed His allegiance. I value Him above any other thing and in the unity, I find prosperity. The Lord is my shepherd, and He leads me with clear unity to supply another the lead of insight gained by His persona. I am ever in the manner of investing in Him my idea making so I intend to flourish with reasoning. I work with the support of His person and in the way of it I am aligned to Him. Showing my honor to Him is wise and I offer it freely. I know I am not the way to eternal standing. It is God alone who is this gift. I in turn rely on Him for all things good and true. I strive to lead where I am placed but it is not for me to say how all things will grow or bloom. I am here as a willing participant who sees the value of God and who orchestrates the love of His counsel to others in need. Sharing the light has meant to be training so another can know God in a personal way. The Scripture I read is good and with hope, so I do not lose my way as I stand in the unity to God. The shared comradery is ever before me. I know to believe I can learn is to garner the gain and move it to others. The less fortunate do not hear as the Great Worker of all is my Savior. In His offered support I enter to the region of knowing where to find the faith and how to be witness to its knowing stand. The claim of God is far more than a solid hope bearing true faith for it offers the completeness of a shared support beam. I have the true knowledge God does not go against a person if they desire to know Him in a favoring light. To lead so others, have the hope I contain is to gift it to the man who yearns to gain in the way of faith. God, the Almighty Caretaker, is my allegiance and support. I know in Him I am given the fruit of the Bible and its contents support all.

My love and training are solid, and I believe I can conquer the hope for many by way of supporting the work of God to the people. My nearness to God is for all time. I will align with care to His heart, so I tread in a way of unity not loss. God is supporting me through the trial of no marriage and a pregnancy in where I am the vested way for man to have eternal gain. How did this come to be for I am mere flesh and bone? God in His professional knowledge knew how to gift me this hope. I would not have known I could be so valued, had God not done this for my stand with Him. He alone is the

Gateway to thrive and know Him with caregiving. I have the unity to push ahead and to witness where He determines my path to follow. I am not the only insight man finds favoring. There are those who have known the King in other connections than what I have been given. We all tell a tale of hope based on our experiences with God. In where man decides who to pursue comes the profession of his belief system. The way of sharing the Bible is a difference for any who know God. Offering light is generous and true not simplistic but hope bearing. It is more than a singular idea for there are many values to the core of knowing God the Creator. He is ever faithful and right. In Him is the necessary support one must have to bear the forthright goal of Him to others. It takes training for this to come into play. I can garner the plan of my own inherit thought process, but no fruit will be in play if I do not have the One who ordained the purpose of it. I walk with the support of sharing the plan so another can hear my own measure of true knowledge. It came by way of the Gospel insight of Scripture. Has the plan been revealed where the Jewish people are tied for all time to God? The bounty of it has been for always. Now the commitment of God is being fulfilled. He is placing me in the mixture so I can spread the favor to another. Did I invite this hope to me personally? I claim the God of man as my own, so it opened the pathway for this to happen. Was it a clear instruction or did I simply imagine it? I read the Scriptures as true hope, and I can see where this process is leading me. I do, however, need to know more for understanding to be given. I invite my God to witness to me, so I conquer fear with hope. In the stand of His care, I am given the faith I need to give others the reward I gained. It is more than a gesture of support for all of me is tied to the One of inspiring gifts. The shadow of no knowledge has lifted, and I enter the gateway of support near to Christ my child. I am ever knowing I shall have to lead with caregiving in such a manner I reflect the support of God to my own ability to flourish. To know I need to be more than the average person is a lie not an insight. No man can be more than another. It is not the way of a man's body but his spirit.

Together with the work of God is the benefit of His counsel. In Him is the support needed to align to His way of thinking. He is spiritual and true. He is glorified where man places the unity to His heart. Why would a person need God if not for the value of hope He presents? There is no greater love than God's offered support. He never fails nor does He gift one no cure for the ailing heart of loss. In Him is the unity man has the capacity to adore. I am here due to the love of God desiring for me to have Him as my own. I unite with Him with caregiving, and we keep as a unity of support and leading in where others are fed true gain. I have the inspiration to deliver a child of great hope and in the manner of it a knowing work is formulated. God is a value non can compare with. It is Him alone who teaches me to thrive and grow in prosperity. With Him as my lead, I shall never fear.

He is generous in favor whereas the falseness of the one of dark impressions has no reward to offer. I enter the faith due to God 's support of my own inherit need. God is far greater than I. I invite Him to support me so I can offer others the knowing way of His caregiving. To know the Word of God is a plan of action that supports the lead of God to me. I have the way of sharing the support and I claim God as my Savior. The true nature of the One who made all of mankind is far more intelligent than any man could be. His ordinance is not one of a small gesture of no imprinting. The value of the King is more than a digested unity. It is all encompassed. I know I am tying my own mind to Him, and I invite Him even more to me. There is never fear for God is a permanent part of my stand. I shall never fear Him for all I know of His character is He never fails my heart. He is rich with hope, and I need His support more than my own life. In eternity I shall be one of the many who found Him righteous and good. Our time here is simply not of the eternal destination. We need to bind to God for the hope of a life of good intentions where we are given favor and true gain. Deception is running in the circle of life and the impression from them leads many to a negative. With the work of God comes the reward of knowing Him in a personal way. I thank Him for His rule of hope and in the way of His counsel I find a witness of pure enlightenment.

> [1] *To man belong the plans of the heart, but from the LORD comes the reply of the tongue.* [2] *All a man's ways seem innocent to him, but motives are weighed by the LORD.* [3] *Commit to the LORD whatever you do, and your plans will succeed. Proverbs 16:1-3 NIV*

God is real to the one who plans for Him to speak to his person. My Lord is the Waymaker who supports my unity to Him for the sake of knowing Him in a personal way. God hears me speak and He offers a plan, so I gain in the support of sharing light. To offer the forward intent so another hears the plan of faith is to align to the Gateway Himself. Sheltering the offered role of impact does not infringe on the heart. It makes it claim God with caregiving. I have the hope God will offer to me a plan in where I know where I am to align to His support through the birth of the Child I carry. How will I know when the time has come to place the knowledge I hold fast to toward the Creator of insight? I shall not have to ponder this for I will gain the way of it from God above. In the creativity of God all things can be performed. I have the value of truth within me, and I work so many find this advantage for themselves. I believe I will hear God tell me where to have the courage to share the Scripture promise of God's gift, so others too hear the insight for their work to prosper. I do not have eternal calling for the love of no offered goal. In the way of sharing the plan of a witness I am tying my unity to above. God is my focal point. He redeems the broken and showers them with the love of His favor. I invite my God to offer to me the lead of an expert witness due to the bounty I carry within me. He has not shown me how to perform this feat, so I wait with caregiving and stand on the manner of who He is to me personally. I share the love and hope of Christ even though He is not within my arms yet. My belly supports the growing way of Him, and this is proof to me I am not without His lead.

Together in God I am tying the support of His person to the one who places value to the Risen I Am. I labor in support of sharing the message of Christ to the man who plans to inherit the unity. God is supportive to me where others are not. I walk currently with courage due to the goal of God within me. I am training to align to the Savior through the knowledge He is my guard. I have the support of some who heard how I came to be expectant of this birth goal, and they accepted I did not have an encounter with a man but with the Holy Spirit. It has taken courage to claim this out loud to mankind. The reward of knowing God protects me is a sign I am valued to Him. The work of God is far greater to me than I realized, and I truly wait with expectation. The reward of planned endeavors has its own merit but when God moves things progress with caregiving. People who have the faith of a mustard seed engage with support to the Creator. They place the work ethic of their hearts and minds into action providing for the many who call God good. I know I will hear from on high where to tread and how to operate. The dual accounting practice of faith and reward have a unity that stands complete. I am with the care of the One who upholds my heart. He supports me to offer others my hope, so they too build with courage. It has taken time for me to learn how to manage where it is difficult and trying. But the Word of God makes things develop where I enter the light with support. The way to share the gift of the Risen Savior is to know what the Word of God has to say. There are verses about the crucifixion and I do not know when this will happen or why, but I place my heart with the One who made me see the goal making. I shelter in the support I know, and I believe God has prosperity for my Child in hand. His birth will bring into the earth a unity not found today. The Gateway is Christ Jesus and He will offer the work in a bountiful way. To learn who the Creator is and how He saw fit to align to me so I can grow in Him is support I vested forth with love. I invite my God to ordain in my way of thinking the right plan, so I do not fail to gain from the action of it. The more I enter into agreement with God the more I can perform with true inspiring goals. I have the insight to read the Book of Faith, and it leads me to discern I am not all-knowing. I am thankful for the opportunity to lead where he places me to, but I am not without His courage and unity, so I act in support and lean into Him with caregiving. It is a gift to know the One who made me as His own.

Christ is the way to thrive and in Him is the fruit of knowing where to step for unity to be had. The secret is not hidden for all of mankind is given the spirit of God. It is the one who places value on it who bleeds with purpose and hope. Caring is part of the mission. In the way of sharing the light comes the reward of support. God invests in the one who portrays the offered goal and spreads it to others. I know man is not always given the opportunity to blend in unity due to his own value being of no inspiration to God. If the hope of a person is to align to God's character a unity will become apparent. The Bible is a record of Christ before He came to earth. In the detail of it man is given the lighted way to know caregiving. I have the hope of giving many others the knowledge I gained. Why would it be a pleasant undertaking? It means the value of God is held within me. I know I am small in comparison to those who studied under the wing of a knowledge professing scholar. Yet, there is the reward just the same as if I had years of reading behind me. The spirit of the living King is bent to sharing the hope forward so all who claim Him are given the option of knowing Him in a personal way. The tie is far greater than of no lead. The offering is not slim or depleted. It is all-encompassing. The witness of the One who made me His own is for the way of Him to prosper me. He enacts the light, and I invest in His caregiving. It shields me from the dark enemy. The One who never fails is God. He is righteous and good to the core of Him. In the way of light is the guarantee He will never hurt me or stand against me if I pursue Him in honoring ways. The witness of a solid, caring intent stands with caregiving quality. The shadow of the moon is obvious when the night sky shines with light from the stars. The Creator hoisted the moon to its point and made the stars give off a glow. Where does a person who has no belief find the courage to offer hope? If no fruit is given what good is a person's value to himself. I shall offer the plan of a witness from on high. The unity I have is far greater than all the wealth I received. I am ever grateful for the light of God within my heart. I know it is a saving measure for me to hear the voice of reason speak. The work of caregiving is not a small gesture nor one of no guiding. It is a tying unity leading to the way of true hope built with support and willing insight. God shares Himself to all. He does not leave any without the option of hearing Him invest in their hearts.

God supports the way to thrive as in Him is the course of hope leading to a better plan. The all-knowing Being of inspiration is one of true moral righteousness. He can adhere to the work of an intent in where time and value are plentiful. God is the way to offer another the goal of sharing Him for the love of insight and growing aptitude. The offer of God is far above that of any other being. God supports the work of His people where He is invited to gift love and goal making. In the support will reside the plan and how to bring it to fruition. The claim of righteous thinking happens where the work is aligned Scripturally, and a solid goal is heard. I know I am given into the pattern of sharing the insight I learned due to the love I carry for this birthing. It is a sign from on high that God is with me. I am not one to believe I claim more than God as my saving witness for He is the Gateway not I. The love of Him is for any who placed value to Him. In His caregiving lives the plan of a man who has the spirit of the saving grace. We are not as He is for we have sin nature; yet He loves us just the same. His cleansing properties are far more than I can tell but I aim to share His value with many. I have the work of His goal making and in the stand of His counsel I am given the support of a genuine lead of wealth. Not the pocketbook kind but the spiritual leading of insight. If I were to declare hope, I have without the experience of His shared bounty who would believe me? No one other than God alone can bring to the heart the reward of His counseling. I am ever in awe of God and who He is to me personally. His care is far above my own ability making. I cannot ascertain one thing without God revealing it to me. He is the great Creator, and I am His subject. To learn and be given the value of God is wrong for no other being is as brilliant. In Him is the factoring of Scripture and spiritual guidance. I shall always be thankful for the thought processes He grants and in the way of them I will bear witness to His good care. I have the work of His call before me so I know I can bear the fruit to another. If I fail it will be due to my own understanding not what God has shown me. I believe I will always have comfort from true worship to Him. He has shown me love and great hope and I enter His presence in a humble manner. I am ever grateful for His counsel as I am mere dust of the earth. Knowing Him is a plan I intend to continue, and I will not move away from His guiding. He is my main reason for life.

The care of God is for me to align to the many who need a witness of hope. I hear the voice of reason, and I discover God is real.

Gift Three

God's Care Is Here

Today I live as one who has the favor of the Most High. In Him is the support supplying my heart with the way forward to thrive. Due to the calling I have been given I am not ashamed for it is God's choosing I will bring life to the One called Savior. Have I had fear? There has been plenty of reason to, yet I stand here knowing God has a purpose for this time. He is not the one to align with no hope. In the manner of me sharing the gift of inspiration I claim God as my lead. He alone is the Gateway to life eternal. By His person man is given the hope of knowing Him in a personal way. He delights in our witness of His caregiving. To be the one who has the Child of hope bearing forward in her inner self means I'm not without insight for God knew I would offer this child the hope I have been given. I awake in the day of true honor, and I perform so others hear of my gain. To know where to offer the light is a reward in where man has the faith to perform so others learn where to give insight. The work of the Mighty Caregiver is always my first idea. In the manner of sharing the offered gain I am committed to reading Scripture even more. I know it feeds me with a preferred lead and in the way of sharing it I bind to God with favor. Can I lead where man is standing in doubt? I can offer the goal I know and build it forward as a significant idea. I am not alone in the offering for God is with me in all I do. He never leaves my side or steps away for a time of discovery. He is faithful and true to my heart as none other can be. Where is the unity offered of mankind if not from on high? The man who has no recognized truth is lost and in the dark with no hope of a dream of light. God revealed His Son in my womb. It came as a surprise for I cannot see as He does. But I am secure knowing I am the right individual to gift this form of delivery to mankind. I work where the door is ajar and, in the insight, value is the idea I can term my goals to His way of being. The power of God is far above my own belief in where I do not invite a false narrative to my plan making. I know the best way to gift others the fruit of my intent is to strive to care as God would. He is the foundation of inspired unity and in Him is the drive I have been gifted. He shall not cause me harm or a false lead. He is great and holy with perfect dream making. I value this gift within, and I look to God for making it happen.

My idea of sharing the light has been a stand I inherited from family before me. I have a lineage where I know my father and mother were tied to the Great I AM. I have history to prove my goal making came from the effort of my dearest relatives. I believe due to being taught I am created by hope not loss. I now offer this knowledge to the Child I carry. I pray over Him with support, and I align Him to the Father. We share in the unity, and it means a good repour between our hearts and minds. God is not like any other thing or being. He can offer me more than a simplistic knowing goal of faith. It is deep with care qualities, and I bind to Him for the goodness of His undertaking. To know the One of the world is watching over me is a sight of knowledge I have been granted. History is for the one who applies and places the work to others. To gift my heart to the man who is in need is what motivates me to stand in caregiving. I look to how God gained me freedom in value, and I share this wealth with thanksgiving. We are not geared to question where the fruit is coming from as we know it is God alone who provides it. I have the knowing aptitude God supports my heart and I offer this to any in need. He is spiritual not of flesh, but this Child I carry shall have arms and legs as I do. I would not be inclined to birth an alien of some sort because this would only prove to be a false identity to mankind. We are united in the way we perform and in the work of God is the plan of hope. For me to carry something other than a child of the Living Word would be false. I would not be determined as secure to know and it would not be wise to look toward this type of narrative. God knows the heart and what feeds it faith. A strange intent is not something of favor for God is orderly and genuine with good leverage for the face of recognition. Knowing the way to attribute the love value of God is a sight of favor one gains by reading the Book of hope. It can be grafted to the heart and stand with care no matter who does the reading. The invitation remains the same for all who apply the Scripture verses to their heart. It does not vary from one to another. The capable way of God is a mighty, significant idea. He is above the wall of deceptive behavior in that He ordains the plan and makes it complete. I have the will of Him within me to gift this Child a lead of inspired goal making. I will offer the knowledge of hope and put it in motion to His daily intake. Whether He is small and frail or standing as a man I shall contribute Him a way of insight. He is not going to need my help, yet I will offer it just the same. Rearing Him is the role I have been given so I will not lose the gift due to no instruction. The Gateway is God not I and I will share this knowledge to all who come before me.

Here is some of Mary's lineage recorded in God's Word.

33 The son of Amminadab, the son of Ram, and of Hezron, of Perez, of Judah, of Jacob, of Isaac, of Abraham, of Terah, and the son of Nahor Luke 3:33 NIV

The lineage of people recorded in early history did not record the woman's heritage, but this is believed to be a witness to Mary's lineage.

My gift to man is not of all-knowing insight for I am merely one who knows her King. I am not given the same properties as other influences from on high. The great way of faith is provided by the One who made me His caregiver. I have the work of God in me, and I know I will align to Him for this is the goal I have. I value my work, but it is not above the lead of the Creator. The Child is more valued than I. He is the Gateway to life eternal and in Him is the reward of salvation. How this is to be determined is for God above to make happen. I work with the support of the One who made me His child. I bear witness to the goal of His call and in the way of it I am fed meaning. I offer my knowing aptitude, but it is not all-encompassed for there is much for me to gain by being tied to the One of hope. In the way of knowing where to align I am given the knowledge God is superior to me over that of other things. No man holds the same value as my God. He is the Gateway, and I am merely the holder of Him. I say this to lead with true hope not to be standing on self-insight. The knowing will have reasoning in this, so I do not invite a false lead to others. I am here due to the value God placed on my heart. The day I committed my yearning to the One of value

I stood in readiness. All of mankind has a role to play where another can learn from his efforts. I look at the gateway presented, and I step in the reward of instructive goals. I am committed to leading where I am given the opportunity to do so. I shall climb the arena of hope for the way of God is bright and with a gain. The work I do is for many to learn of the expectation I have been given. The Child I deliver will offer man the work of His heart and in the way of it man will be granted a better unity to Christ.

I tie to the One of brilliance and honor. He is the Gateway for me to learn and develop with character. His power is for all to learn by. Should I not believe He is ever with me for the purpose of knowing me as His own? No other cares as deeply for my care in life. To know the One of hope is a stand I adhere toward. I work to offer another the role of inspiring leadership. The salutation of honor comes to the man who achieves the unity and who ascertains He is righteous. I know I am not one to lose my perspective. I care for the lead I offer. It is significant in that it stands as a hope for others to learn of God. The inherit role I have been given is not for all to have the work of God for not all of mankind believes God is the lead in his own life witness. I place value to God. He ordains my timing, and I bind to the one working with caregiving. It can be a simple lead of hope in the form of writing a note or speaking in a framework of true knowledge. You can adhere to someone with care in many ways. I know caregiving is a sight of birth this Child will need. I do not act out of haste where I gain no important knowing aptitude. I work to learn and gain knowledge of Scripture. It takes the heart, the will to share the light before hope is gifted to another. If you invite God to align to you so rewards come, and prepare for others to know who is the Great I AM you are sharing the way forward to the one with no insight. The value of a witness is supportive if God is the focal point. The lead of Christ is far above any other unity present in this life.

I speak with support from on high. The goal I share is for man to find the light and spread it to others near them. I shower my God with unity, and I enter His way of being due to the love I have for His person. He is the gateway I have been bonded to. I value the light of God and in the way of Him I am fed the value of hope instilled with knowing He is ever with me. I act as one, but He is within me. I share the love I have been given, and glory resides in making my heart to God. It is a goal I placed for my own undertaking. I look at where I have been favored and I see the support with courage. I know I am never without the draw and support due to the love God has for me. In the way of the hope I am gifted, I honor the Savior with care. I am tied to this Child I carry, and I enjoy the way of God to me. I shall never speak ill of God for He is the Great I AM. The Word of Scripture teaches me I am valued and supporting to man. I know to offer the plan of a witness is to declare God is superior to me. I do not plan to align to the false presence for it has no unity to me. Dark thoughts are not something I adhere to. I am here standing in unity to the One who made me right and true. Am I ever to have my own inherit stand? No, because I choose to walk with the Lord. He builds me the way forward and in Him is the faith for a righteous King. God knows me and He guided me to support others in need. I walk with the unity of God's care. I shall not lose my thought processes of hope as I know how to reward my offered insight. I stay in the mix of God the Father, and I learn from Him how to operate. The lead of God is not slim nor is it without the support I need to flourish. My guidance Counselor is the Word of Christ as He is and always has been present. I work to offer others the fruit I have been given and in the way of sharing the light my work is supportive to another. The offered gain is a witness I know means value. God is my Waymaker not I. I offer the love and care due to the realization God granted me the work ethic. I know the way to offer hope is built with the unity God provides me. I bear forthwith true intent, and I lead so others can know God as I do. To work so another has the belief, and the option of gain is why I enjoy reflecting forward the hope. The favor is a gift, and the work of my hand is not as Christ, but I am tied to Him in faith. He shows me where to align and how to witness with courage. The battle is not my own but rather of God, the one of brightness.

Glory is given to the one who faces hope and witnesses its courage. The power of God is not a gift for only the believer but for all who call on His name. But the unity will not blossom, nor will the effect be right if no value is given to God. I know I am not one to bloom if no hope is present. I maneuver so others can find the fruit I have. It has taken time to be mature enough to lead and in the manner of it I claim God above all else. The shoulder of hope is from Him alone. He is the Gateway I needed to learn and find out where to step. The faith I have is not simplistic. It bleeds the beauty of God and His person is within me. Is the hope of Him for all of mankind? I believe it to be true. I look at where the value is given. I know God is ever faith bearing. With Him is the hope for man to flourish and stand in an upright way. Do I ever fear or lose hope? At times it can happen. Then I am guided to the light of Christ and lean into Him for support. This Babe I carry is all-encompassing. He is ever bright and good. Will I know Him for always as I do the Father? Yes, the hope is claimed in them as one Being of sight. They are separate but not without the will of the Spirit working within them. The love of God is for any who believe and shine with caregiving qualities. I value the heart and the one who performs for others to gain. I endear to the way of God, and it is all I trust. Many have fallen prey to the work of their hands, and it stands as no reward. Do I invest where I am not welcomed? I wait to see whether God supports me to do so. He is a calm way of being. He does not force His way to any who do not desire Him. Why would another choose to pursue Him if they had no hope in Him? He is always the way to thrive even if one is perishing this is understood. God values my intent and in Him is the way to prosperity. I know I am not the slight being I used to be. Due to the option of learning where the light is bestowed, I claimed the way to thrive and be standing with caregiving. The saving reward I found is far greater than the long wait time I have seen in the past as God is always giving support. God supports the one who places value to His care. I have known the bounty and gain due to belief and support to Him. The work of my heart is not slim. I retain the Word due to repetitive reading and hearing the voice of God in my mind. I look at what I hear and place value to the light. If a dark thought brings a claim, I know it is false and do not engage. One who places a negative to prosper is a person with no insight. Looking at the voice of hope is a way of support many have not yearned to know. Why this happens is not something I can relate to. God is so intent on me being a good influence He gave me a precious gift of hope. I gain in the plan and in the way of sharing Him I learn too.

The support of knowing how my God works far outweighs the hope of man to me. The lighted path is far more in abundance than the invested way man leads. I have the unity to know what is genuine and what is daydreaming.

God puts forth a plan of inspiring gifts that abound with perfect witness making. Does it mean all you believe will perform as you think? No, for God is greater than the inspiring of self. To perfect a goal and put it into action so others learn from it is far greater than all the control of the bounty. The suture to man is the way he believes on high. I work with the Lord's best thought processes. How do I know this is true? I look to where my faith is found. I stand on the principal way God offers His manner to mankind. In Scripture it is nourishing hope needed to offer others a better way of life. Should I believe I have the only way forward? No, for I do not see what the Savior does. I bank on the fact God offers me a dream and I can align to Him with a vested interest. His capital may require more than I envision, and the growing way of His goal may be a light burden or one of significance. I do plan to offer what I am given in a sure way of support. This may be a simple offering or one of many ideas. It takes the heart the planning to invest so I dream with purpose. I act where the door presents so I know I am in the workings of God. I do not force my hope forth for that only brings no reward. I know to offer others a better life is support I aim to invest. I am not rich with monetary holdings, so I gain in other ways. I pray and offer the vested way of my labor. I do not hold all the ability to thrive on my own. I need others to align to God just as I am. In the reward we value the whole investment not just one singular way.

The circumstances of my situation came because of my intent to offer God my only way of being which is to follow Him in support. He had a goal for my heart to learn of His caregiving nature. I am tied to Him personally so I know I will be protected in the way of this journey. I do not know the plan or how it will come to be; yet I offer my heart to Him with unity. In sharing this gain, I too am given the lead of hope to give to another. I know I am not the only person to have a trial to be put through. God is not one to do harm. Man does this action and in the way of it others fall short or lose insight. The commitment from on high is I will have support through the stand. I take this as courage to my heart. I have the value of the Spirit of truth so I know I will learn and grow with wise understanding. The way of Christ is yet to be heard but I know from Scripture it will come to pass. I am honored to share faith with others who learn of my goal. I am to stand on behalf of a babe of hope and in the way of this I will invest my own body and time. My counterpart is not man but the Savior. He will lead me with courage, and I will know Him as my Lord. I perform the role of teaching in where others see me align to God. It stands as the measure of me not God for man is not holy or right without the Father's care to his counsel. I am committing no harm or lie in where the offering I am holding is from on high. It is hard for some to grasp God is indeed doing as He said He would. Bringing forward the gift of His own self so man can know Him as Savior. Work is for the one who places value in the offered faith. I am tying my heart to the baby within me, and I know I will offer Him my own identity so He can align to God in a solid unity. My heart is standing on the plan of God not my own undertaking. The lead of Jesus will be to call to man and if he pursues Him a bond of good intent will be handed to him. I have taken the knowledge of God and applied it to me in a personal way. The love of Christ is far more valued than my own merit for I am not as He is. I have no special powers or ability set apart from any other human. I am merely willing to offer my heart and mind to the love value of the Risen I AM. I speak where the heart is tied, and this is the favor I found. It leads me to the quest for a solid goal, so no harm befalls the way of my child rearing time. I work with care as God directs, and I aim to be partnered to Him in respect not lordship. He is far greater than I will ever be. I offer this knowing I will one day speak to Him in person and teach Him my own words of wisdom. For He is about to be a baby in my arms not a man of strength. It won't mean He can't perform for He will be God in unison to His fleshly body. How this will be it is for Him alone to decipher. I thank my God for the opportunity to align to Him with this outreach. Will I ever be the site plan to offer the way forward? Only in that aspect can I voice what I gain from the truth of Scripture.

My lead is a gentle whisper due to hope with insight for the Word of God has spoken to my heart. I now hold the plan of salvation within me, and I learn from the process what is to be. I do not know the future for only God has this knowledge. I work to guard the knowing attributes of faith, so I adhere with a ready lead. I am a woman so this must be done in the proper order. I do not engage with the partner of another who is male for it is not wise to do so. A woman has the gift of sharing spiritual knowledge by way of her experiences from on high. Her knowing work is what sets in motion a value due to the witness of her life. Many have the heart to lead but not all are gifted in doing it. I am not male, so I work with the knowing ability my history is what stands as insightful. I am not the work of an author for writing is not my plan. I am not a scholar nor am I one to teach in a classroom. That support is for the male path to follow. Times change and I know one day this may not be the case but due to this generation I will follow the goal of my heritage. Leading is a submissive unity in that the role of the worker must fit the outreach. In the plan of salvation, it is God who has the power, it is not I. I work in other forms. Reading the truth brings with it an abundance of gain in where I aim to live as a righteous wife. My knowing manner will provide the recognition necessary to align to God's support. In the way of sharing the lead of my heart I will invest with care offering those in my pathway the gain I have been gifted. I know I am not the Creator nor am I the way for hope to be given. It is my investment to God that binds this connection value. He leads me to speak and offers me the wisdom of when to be silent. I claim God is far more than I for a reason. He is the source of a righteous caretaker where I am the one learning from Him. He stands as my guidance counselor, and I invite His wisdom to me. I learn and grow with favor due to His moral righteous way not my own.

Right goals mean to align with hope to the Lord and His way of being. I offer the knowing aptitude that God is a value I cannot maintain, nor can I perform as He always does. I am working to gift to another the lead I have known. But in the way of sharing, I sometimes fail. I look to the work of others to learn too. Do I have all the knowing capacity of all of man? No, for I am merely a young guide. Many others applied longer study habits than I have, yet God chose me just the same to align to Him in support. I know He will do this for all who believe and work on His behalf. It may require some insight value outside of direct communication to the Master. God ordained man to train one another for the benefit of His calling. I lead to align to Christ, the One who offered me my goal making. How does it happen if not by His leading? I shall never know all there is to learn for I am not educated as a guidance counselor nor am I the way to life eternal. The Spirit of the Living Word is my lead. I follow it with support knowing

I am the offered hope to carry the birth and life of Christ. It is for man to believe in not for me to force the issue. If no one had the courage to train where would offering insight come from? God is a planner. In Him is the correct way of thinking. Man is a witness on His behalf. He trains to guide from the Scripture verses contained in the Word of God and in the way of this training good thoughts build. I know I am not the gift to man that my baby will be. He alone is the gateway for all to gain entry through the passage of heaven's doorway. Leading is significant as sharing the love and the vision of support leads to man finding the path of insight. It is real and good to process and in the way of thinking in an upright way nurturing develops where faith is given. Aspiring leads to transforming the spirit and in making this way good intent is forward to the mind. I shall never walk away from the gift of unity God provides. It offers too much freedom in the form of support and guidance. I shall always know my saving grace comes from on high.

16 *"For God so loved the world that he gave his one and only Son, that whoever believes in him shall not perish but have eternal life. 17For God did not send his Son into the world to condemn the world, but to save the world through him. John 3:16-17 NIV*

Our teaching to others, gifts support and knowing aptitudes of light. The reward is a sight of birth I intend to complete till the process of sharing has been fulfilled. Who can hear and gain, is not for me to know. It is God who masters the draw and sets in motion the aptitude of knowing Christ and His manner. Is there room for error when I take into consideration the timing of things? By God's power I will not fail. He alone gifts the right things to say and what is to be heard. I have the work of God within me, and I learn from the Scriptures where to give others the unity. In making a singular idea much faith can be granted. I realize I am not the great way of life. I have limited abilities, and I lean toward God for the hope I have. I am tying my heart and mind to His caregiving. In the way of knowing what is valued I too am fed the spiritual gain necessary to align to God with purpose. I work with an intent to administer the gain, so others find the work favoring. Is there a stand for me to witness that I haven't been unified to? I do not hold all the value. I merely try to train those willing to learn the unity I have. I look at what the purpose is given and I judge whether it is right or good. In sharing the light, I now have the notoriety I am not smitten but rather God is the one who receives the blessing of fame. I too shall be known for carrying the Christ Child, but I am not Godlike nor am I as righteous as He is. I will not accept the provision of master when it is not I who aims to claim all of mankind to the heart of Himself. I merely possess the value of God not the entirety of His support. He has far greater strength in the way of a righteous lead than I shall ever hold. I know I tie to Him in faith due to reading the Work of His making. But I aim to offer this gift just the same. The way to place value to the One of inspiring standing is to offer your counsel to those in need. It can be simple or complex. A note of encouragement or a daily practice of sharing Biblical insight can be the knowledge for another. I now realize I don't have to push forward an agenda for God has the way prepared for me. I am not one to offer an exterior of no fruit. It is not worthwhile to do this kind of growth. I claim God for the good He is to me, and I share this knowledge in a way of light to the heart. I give freely the knowledge I speak and in the way of this gifting others will know God for themselves. Learning to pray has been a blessing to me. I know I will always talk with the purpose of knowing God in a personal way. It comes as a sign of faith. The work of Scripture to me is not without support so tie to the blessed Being of gain and turn to Him with favor.

The unity of feeding the sheep of the One who made all mankind is a gift of inspiring leading. I am shelter to the man who places his calling toward Christ. Is there a goal to share in this? I believe there is in that I know I am binding the will of God to others. This Child is my own gift to me. I am not the way of mankind to thrive or gain in factors outside of a witness of faith, yet, in the way of my heart is the reasoning God is genuine and holy. I have the Scripture grounding to align to the right manner of favor due to implementing God to my heart. I shall offer to man the reason I have for growing in faith. It comes by way of light not dark thought processes. To know the way to offer the guiding established goal is to develop the way to gift meaning to someone. In the manner of knowing the faith and how it comes into play is to align to God in perfect wisdom. I have the hope of knowing who is the great I AM and in Him I shall witness much reward. He created me to know Him, and I believe He is my all in all. Every day I look to hope as He granted me the will to follow Him in faith. I have not fallen into the trap of fear, yet, at times I endure hard times. Does this mean God has forgotten me or that He doesn't care? No, He is ever with me in the trying time. He guides me with courage, and He shields me with support where I know I am given a return of gain. To know God is supportive of my intent is for me to realize I am giving myself to Him in a free manner. There are no chains holding me in tow. He is the light, and I lean toward it in favor. I enjoy a story of hope and the Word of God supports this in me. I took up reading Scripture from Him with a unity of inspiring trust. I have the work of God in the inner self, and I am alive with care due to it. I shall call man to Him in the way of sharing the lead I have been given. The work of God is to gift mankind the power to know Him personally. Why is this important to Him? He created man in His own image and in making him He granted man the ability to decide for himself who he would pursue.

[27] So God created man in his own image, in the image of God he created him; male and female he created them. Genesis 1:27 NIV

My knowing gift is to share the light and to offer the measure God provided me with. I am slight with no hope if I believe I am the Gateway of life for I merely support God I am not He. I contribute my lead to His power and in the way of life I know He expresses me toward His person. He is generous and good and in the manner of knowing Him I am given support leading to an experience of favor. To know God is to develop a lean into His caregiving qualities. He supports me with care and I intake His calm presence knowing He is the way to life with true gain. The way of God is clear and encouraging to me. I know He is the one who ordains my heart and claims it as His own. In the shadow of Him I can be heard. To know the light is from His care means to me to be holding faith within my heart. I look to His counsel to know where and how to gift others the knowing aptitude of His well intending unity. If you value to know life gain but are missing the hope it is due to no intent of being tied to God in a personal way. He alone is the sacred bond I experience. He is the great I AM, and I now have His Son in my own flesh. Did I ever invite God to birth His Child within me? No, I only made myself willing to grow in Him. He chose me for a purpose which is yet to be determined by Him alone. I do not have power, nor will I ever be the way to life eternal. A false acceptance would be to claim I am more than that. I shudder to think one might have the idea I am more than another. I am delicate and made of good favor due to the witness of God to me. I have the bond of God, and I align to His person. Should I fear being His offered role model? I intend to perform for God the Father in a way this Child will learn the value of who He is. I know there are those who seem to assume I have something outside the normal body, but this is false and with no right thinking. I am not the way ahead that is God Himself. He is ever available to all who call on Him in faith. I look to God for knowing gain and in the manner of Him I find support. I could not walk this path on my own merit. I have sin nature as all mankind does so I am not holy or justified without God's work in me. I thank the Lord for His support, and I will offer others the way of hope simply by witnessing who Jesus is to me. He is the Gateway not I nor will I ever be.

My heart is not simplistic but of true hope in God filled with the goal of knowing Him in a personal way. I have the plan of His caregiving quality and in the way of knowing Him I am fed support. To align to His person prepares me with committing His holy stand. I am given the value of His heart and in the committed hope from His counsel I gain in the unity. He ties me to Him, so I enter His presence with clear gain. I am not one to offer no hope as God provided me with the reward of knowing Him. I evaluate the manner of His intent and in the way of His spiritual leading I witness His support. The way to align to Him is to pray and feed on Scripture which is a guarantee of sharing the bounty He provides. I am not the way to know Him. It takes the effort of oneself for this to happen. I gained the hope of His support in that I know I am one of His children. The bride spoken of in the Biblical sense is the sight I intend to portray. Pure longing is my investment, and I look to where the work of God takes my heart. I am willing to learn and to offer another the pathway due to knowing the benefit of it. I share where the door is ajar and in the way of united faith I gain the reward. I lead if the unity is rich and, in the work, I commit a role of faith. The work of my hands is for all to learn and to be presented the honor of sharing the birth of God to another. I evaluate the opportunity, and in the bond, I tie with courage. I offer the role I gain to any who knows the way to prosperity. Work is pleasant due to my own idea of it being for God. He supports my idea making and He favors me withstanding. Should I learn just for the value of His support? He grants me the idea and if it is something I am willing to offer another I step forth with courage and hope. In the way of God man has hope from the Bible and how to grow with insight. I am the reason others gained what I know. The example I portray is not slim nor is it insignificant. I team with the Savior, and I grant others the hope I have known. Never have I been without His guiding for He supports me. As a young person I learned to follow Him with hope being my insight. God is my all in all and I gift to Him my value system. I shall not step outside of His glory, nor will I lose my inspiring aptitude. He is ever faithful to my witness.

Care is from the One who made me His own. I am valued and, in the gift, I spread harmony. I believe no other has the power to feed my spirit with such courage and hope. I maintain the level of scrutiny due to the way I came to be invested with this pregnancy. I am not the all-knowing Being of insight, but I am the way for many to learn who the Savior will be. I have the birth to claim Him before the marriage to Joseph, and he chose to stand with me on this journey. God spoke to him, so he knew I was not capable of betraying his love. I am never going to say I am without hope as God is ever with me in this idea of favor. I did not ask for such a blessing, but it is my honor to allow it to happen within me. I accepted the value of God, and I took Him to me in a personal way. I can offer mankind the plan of salvation, yet I do not understand how it will happen. I place my faith in the palm of God's knowing I am with His person while working to gift others the unity I know. From the perspective of sharing light, it is a reward I adhere to. I am not insignificant, but I am as any man for I am not as God. He is the way the truth and the life. I place value to the Creator and He alone is the Gateway to life eternal. Knowing who made me is a gain in where I offer my heart to Him in thanks and support. God is my delight! I believe He will grant me the knowledge when the time is at hand to do so. He will always know more than I and this is good for me. In the way of it I shall never lose my perspective that He alone is the great I AM.

[18] This is how the birth of Jesus Christ came about: His mother Mary was pledged to be married to Joseph, but before they came together,

she was found to be with child through the Holy Spirit. [19] *Because Joseph, her husband, was a righteous man and did not want to expose her to public disgrace, he had in mind to divorce her quietly.* [20] *But after he considered this, an angel of the Lord appeared to him in a dream and said,* [21] *"Joseph, son of David, do not be afraid to take Mary home as your wife, because what is conceived in her is from the Holy Spirit. She will give birth to a son, and you are to give him the name Jesus, because he will save his people from their sins.* [22] *All this took place to fulfill what the Lord said through the prophet.* [23] *"The virgin will be with child and will give birth to a son, and they will call him Immanuel"- which means, "God with us." Matthew 1:18-23 NIV*

My way is not to team without the One of insight. In growing and sharing the hope I know comes the favor of God to me personally. I know I am not the Almighty Caretaker. He alone is the respected light found in the truth of the Word. I read to align my heart to His calling. If I sleep in growing it, I shall not find prosperity. The work of God is for me to stand on not gift to myself. To guide another in the calm of God is to know Him with good support. The community I live in is a way to gift man more knowledge. I grow with care, and it is right for me to witness this to others here where I reside. I do not enter the stand of no prosperity, but I am not a wealthy woman. I have an investment in the way I perform, and it is with this courage that true honor is given. I have the work of the Caretaker and in Him is my support. I do not plan to give my favor to any who do not choose to hear it because this would only mean a loss to me in a personal way. I realize man must choose for himself who he will follow and how he will align his goal making. To learn where to stand is something all must declare for their own self. I am not the way to thrive, but I can point you in directing who is. It is for man to decide who he will claim. We all have the insight within us as to who is truly the great Master of all, yet man often fails to remain in this goal making. Where does this come from? I believe it is the enemy of Christ who draws man to him in place of the Gateway of hope. It isn't the All-knowing who steps away for He values all of mankind. He shepherds the lead of the weak and provides a plan for them to prosper all the while delivering on faith. It takes the heart to be intended for the faith to bloom. I know the unity is written in care and I can align with God, and I take it to heart this is where I choose to find insight. The great One of favor is my hope. He never leaves me alone or without the aid I need to thrive and grow in faith. A developed individual is not one who stands in the way of another to learn. It is the man who places value to those around him so they too can inherit the opportunity he claims.

My offered role of mother to the Christ child is far greater than I anticipated. I knew God would work within me I just didn't believe it to be as this is. Am I here to boast about it? Never! God is sympathetic of all His people, and He works with the one who portrays true knowledge in Him. If you offer your heart to God, He will align to you a plan of hope, so you engage with value not pride. The work of God is for man to know Him in a personal way. I have the dream of sharing Scripture so many find the Word of God supportive to them. I claim the way I act due to the gift I have been given. Will there be an incentive for me to allow another to perform with clear intent coinciding with good favor? If I am to uphold in the way of counsel, I will need aid from on high. The blessed gift of this birth is not lost to me. I know I am here for a purpose. It is clearly more than I anticipated but I gain in the way of it. All of man will learn of this Child and I will be noted as being His guardian. Should I accept this without consequences? There are always those who don't endear themselves to God, so they'll fight my stand and tear away the fabric of my word, but I don't fear, God has me protected in His caregiving. The way of knowing where to align comes by way of sharing the light of the One who intends for you to offer hope forward. It is value and standing where hope resides. I am not the way but the bearer of this gift. I should not offer a false lead because it would stand against the Risen I AM. I have the work of knowing my insight being from God due to the many training hours I placed before Him. It came from studying the Scriptures and knowing the intent is for my heart to know God. I value my God, and I am tying Him to me with support. The Word of God is far greater than anything I read in other forms. I learn where to offer my plan and how to ordain it so others can gain a witness for their own undertaking. Shall I lose my salvation or worse try to retain no hope and goodness? What would that gain me? There is only one good stand to work from and that is God's point of view.

My offered role of leading is to invest where the Lord places me. I may travel and grow in unity to the manner of others in a new region. Is this the way for me to perform so others hear the support I found? Anywhere can be the objective to witness. The burden is God's not mine. He is the way to grow and gain hope. In His value system I have the bounty and the retention to thrive and grow spiritually. I am tying the love value He has to the mind of my own understanding. I light the forward way by witnessing the reach of my hand to another. It may mean I must advance in the offered hope in some form I have not recently received. The growth is not of small, insignificant leading due to the One I follow. God is glorious and true. He is the Gateway I hope to learn by. I have the Scriptures to read, and I gift them forward in my actions to those around me. I now realize I am tying my heart to the care of God in my speaking of the hope I carry. Should I invest in any other offering where there is little to term as holy? Even if it meant a great deal of wealth I would not lead in this fashion. The main reason to learn is to gain the hope of God into your manner of livelihood. It has taken me by surprise in where I did not know how God would work in me. I stood willing and that made the difference. Did I look for such a reward to come to me? No, I simply declared to God I was in His camp, and I would work for Him if He chose to use me. I grow with each passing day, so I know I am bringing life forward. I know I did not make this unity rather God above was the intended goal. He is the reason for all to know life eternal. The work of sharing a favor of this magnitude carries with it the knowledge I am worthy only due to God choosing me not my own actions. I am the same as any other person in that I have sin nature. I am not pure without blemish.

God pours Himself into my heart. I invited Him to me with prayer and learning Scripture. Does it mean I won't make a mistake or step into loss if I assume too much of myself? I am made of flesh as any other human is so there is a chance it can happen. Training so I aim forward in the path of righteous walking is my intent. It is the training I have been getting so I evolve with care not my own idea making. God supports me in the way I offer to another His lead. I can say I am not at loss to another due to the reasoning I apply truth to my goal making. I have the reward of sharing the plan of hope and in this idea, others gain a witness too. To know where to thrive comes into play and offering it is not simplistic. God is greatness not harsh ideas of no lead. If you have the goal of a Biblical plan realize God is at work showing you how to benefit others with caregiving. I learn and in the way of it I am fed spiritual witness making. Does this mean I always know where to align to others? I merely offer what I know and let God gift the gain. I have little wealth, yet I am tying man to the Mighty One of prosperity. All the gifts of saving others are not my work but of God. He is the Gateway of spiritual context in where man finds the Gateway of hope. Jesus will be the way forward to know the Father. In His stand man will have an abundance he has not yet gained. The lead will carry far into the future for there will be no end date where God is not the value to all life. I am not the way to offer hope, but I do know who will be. This Child I carry will know my heart and He will offer to me a better pathway to His witness. I shall carry this Babe and gift it to God for He is the Father to Him. Knowing this is right and good makes it easy to believe I am well intending. Have I the ability to know the future where man will give himself to Christ? No, I merely assume the plan will be of a true gain. I have the work of God in me, and I know He is right and true so this will not change. He alone is the unchanging Being of insight.

[8] *Jesus Christ is the same yesterday and today and forever. Hebrews 13:8 NIV*

My gift is to witness to those who hear my work and believe in this Child as the Gateway of life.

The value of God is not weak nor is it a small holding of no hope. God is the true bond of man to His partnering in favor. I have a way of sharing the light and in the manner of it I am given over to hope. The reward is all-encompassed. I thank my Lord for the work I have been given. To bear the Baby of love is not a small investment. I know I am tying man to the way of God and in Him is the hope for all to learn the way for life eternal. I am not the height nor breath of God for He alone is the Gateway of value. I have the support of the Waymaker and in Him I am fed unity. To know the One of creation is to believe in Him in a personal way. I do not declare this to be forthright without true knowledge as the Bible is clear to the believer. If you have the hope of knowing the God of mankind but do not apply the faith you are not one of His children. You merely have head knowledge of who He is. I learn by reading the Book of Hope. It is by this learning I feed my spirit the value of God. To personally place my whole being into the hands of the Savior means I accept His counsel even though it may sting my consciousness. I have the unity of favor and in the way of it I bind to God with care. He is the way to learn insight and to place value to others. I look at who claimed me as His own and I have no other influence that directs me to stand with support. Man is simplistic with little bounty in where God is all-knowing. He alone is the plan of hope and in Him is the drive to live in abundance. Where is the hope if not in favor of Him? None can ordain the spirit and claim it to him. Only God can align man to His support. The reward is to know God and to place value in His counsel. I have the gift of studying and in the way of it I am fed delight. Caring is a gift, and, in the unity, I share the value. I gain in where I tie my heart to God in faith. His guiding is far greater than the smallness of favor from man. Man acts for self alone where God instructs one to witness for the value of others. It is not a simplistic setting where no one can find hope. With the patience of sharing the unity I claimed God as my own shareholder. I look to offer another reward I found and in doing this action faith brings gain to others. I value my Savior and, in His step, resides the witness of value all need to accomplish a plan of hope withstanding any trial. Leading is not for the faint of heart. It takes the spiritual leading to align so another can hold the witness of faith. I am not the Gateway who delivers the plan, but I intend to gift what I know to another in need.

My work is not slim for I carry the precious One of true honor. I am not the goal but the delivery mechanism. Does the Word say I am more than any other? No, it speaks to me as the bridge for birth to happen. I did nothing to receive this honor I merely placed value to God. He witnesses my shouldering of hope and knew I would accept the reward offered with care. Did I believe I would be this gifted? No, for I am not unique or groomed more than any woman of today. The manner of me obtaining this goal came by way of prayer to God and the willingness to align to His call. Did I prepare for it? I was not of ill repute and stayed free from offering my body to man, but I am still with sin nature just as all women are. I have not spoken to the many who speak of my regard as being false. I am not in line to value this kind of payment. God will protect me as I carry forward and work on His behalf. Will the Baby I carry be given a false hold? I do not believe God will do this kind of witness for He values His Child as I do. Man will talk and speak without knowing the truth for this happens every day, but I am here standing on the principle I am not the gift but the one who bears witness to Him. I love my Child and in Him is the stand of inspired goal making. He leads me with pure value, and I offer my own identity by way of bearing this growth of hope so man can have eternal life to God. I am not the Almighty nor will I ever be. I am not the gold to man but the one who carries it in her womb. The distinction is large. I am value only in that I offer the faith to my fellow people in that I align to God and His offered role for me. I am not the builder nor am I the Gateway to life. God alone is this beacon of saving power. I am trained to share the message of true unity and in doing this action I claim God as genuine. He does not deceive nor will He ever. He walks in an upright position and in doing so He never fails. He is above man in He holds the knowledge needed to be significant in all He does. Man is simplistic. He fails and loses the reward of his own understanding as he does not always have the answer to life. I know I am not above another and in this knowledge, I view God as the eternal gift. He supports me and I look to Him for my witness. I am nothing without His hand on me.

The growth and opportunity to thrive is ever before my heart due to the value of the King I hold fast to. I am tying my efforts to Him in hope and prosperity. I have the value of knowing where He leads so I engage in His manner not that of no control or insight. He works with the unity we share and in making good work hope is built. I am not without a few misgivings at times for all of mankind feels this at times. Yet, I know I am given the value of God due to the way He guides me to offer hope to others. I share the unity of knowing the way He manages, and in His counsel, I learn to offer hope. I do not need to see the future as the way God operates is holy and true. I know He will not feed me little support as in Him is the wealth of a league of many. He holds the vested way to life and in Him is my plan of insight. I follow Him with the manner of sharing a reward so another can find the faith I have been supported with. Is there a need to pray and be given a sight plan from it? I know God works when I realize what I need to do to gain the way I hope to achieve. It comes by way of vision planning, not my own understanding. There is a tying of hope with it, and it blesses me to pursue the term of it. In the manner of sharing the hope I have been given I turn to God and find Him favoring my idea making. How this portrays to others is not my value but rather the need to gift others what I learn. The commitment happens and I work for the better of the idea to be shared to those who are willing to gain from it.

The study of a shared insight can be of a simple idea and how to make it thrive. It may be simplistic, or it may be genuine and in need of others to make it prosper. I envision a goal and ask the heavenly Father how to achieve it, so He offers to me the plan. If no insight is witnessed, I assume I have more in-depth knowledge to learn and I work in this fashion. I know I am not the way to learn but I share how I witness and develop the knowing way to prosperity. It takes the heart time to determine what it wants to be like. In the manner of sharing the faith I lean into others so they too can have the bounty I am given. It takes planning and a vested way of working so man can learn where to align his idea making. Will there always be a way ahead for me to work toward? God has given me ideas in a plentiful way, so I share what I learn to the one seeking an advantage in the same manner. I do look at what happened in the Book of knowledge to recognize how God gifts man the needed work ethic to stay standing in His counsel. Money can bring a person to their knees and cause him to lose his walk with Christ. So, I act in accordance with the need He governs sharing where I can the righteous way of attending in harmony to His call. Should I believe I am without blemish or sin? No, for all mankind has this within him. I know many find me a pure emblem due to being gifted the Child of hope, yet, this is a false idea. No human is solid in his own way. He needs the love and salvation of God to be one of hope or light. To place your own value to your witness is false and should not happen. I do not work so others know me, but rather so men will be known by Christ. I am not the Gateway, nor will I ever be. I know I am tying some to the quest of sharing my heart, but this is not to be. It is God who is the pure One not I.

The reward of sharing the hope comes to the heart and the spirit of man where the love of God is invited to be. The order of hope is not slim nor is it without the reward of gain. I am expressive in the way of knowing who created me and how He intended me to operate. I value the role of knowing who the King of man shall be, yet I am here in wondering it as you have been. I do not see into the way of the all-knowing as I am mere flesh and bone. God is above me in a far greater presence. I work to know Him, so we stay connected and with a unity one to another. I am not the singular Being of insight for only God is this description. I tie to the Gateway as all who profess Him in faith do. I am not the gift to mankind for that alone is Jesus, my Child. He is the Gateway all need to learn where to grow in favor and find the knowing way of life. Is this new for you to learn? Many believed due to my pregnancy being of unnatural circumstances I am more than another. What a false belief! I learn as any other human does and in the way of it God supported me to be the woman who declares the value of Him to others. I learn as another human, and I bleed as one. There is no super power I have other than God above supporting me. I invite the work of God to me and in this way, I am fed support. Do I ever find a viewpoint where I am alone in this offered unity? At times I am weak, and I fail to believe how great my God can be, but this is not the norm for I gained the knowing way to align to God. Scripture is the unity belief maker. If you are trying to gain but there is no alternative before you that springs forth as good, you are not tying to the Gateway of hope. You merely desire a plan not the investing God. Should this come to you as a surprise? God wants mankind to share in Him with unity so He won't pressure you to reach out and call on His name if you don't offer Him your whole presence and spirit of love. He is ever on call if you are so inclined so know He will always hear you if you believe and speak to Him in care.

Gift Four

The Savior is Creation's Light

To know God is to declare Him as holy. The lead of the One who made mankind has been a source of revenue since man was created. How man came to be is recorded in Genesis and the account of it stands complete. We are not all-encompassing. We align to the Great I AM not Him to us. Man can be fed a little of God or an inspiring amount based on faith. The value of God is far more important than any dream for building in favor. How one applies his hope is what sets forth the unity and how it looks to the Gateway of hope. God knows if He is the offered reward or if He is merely a ticket to more wealth and leading. Spiritual benefits come by the hand of the Father not man to man. When one supports God, he places value to Him in the way of sharing the hope so others too can achieve the plan of knowledge. If you prosper but have no faith in God, it comes directly due to your own initiative which means nothing on judgment day. God supports the work of man but if it is all he invests in where is the hope found? I know firsthand man can complement his own heritage. The Bible records many who fell short due to their own intent not of God's. It may be all you need is a broom and a mop to be in the vested way of God's care. Do you have a contented way of operating or are you driven to stand on the witness you are making? I know God is a value to me so throughout the course of a day I aim to have a witness to Christ in prayer and speaking to Him in support. Work is secondary to my lifestyle. I work so I can have a home and my needs accomplished but I don't need a level of wealth that causes me to lose my witness in a holy manner. Goals are not always great to achieve for at times it may be they cause more loss than insight. To know the limits of your plan is wise and true wealth. God can bring much favor if that is all that holds you to Him but when the final day of life comes into play you may not have been gifted unity to God and that is a shallow offering. Where God is the great One of faith is where He is the focal point to your heart and mind. Take time to offer Him the reward of your outlook and know He is the Gateway to life. It matters how you tend to Him in your viewpoint and what it is that witnesses to your spirit. Work so others learn where you contribute your plan and know God will favor you when you apply your goals to His way of thinking.

[1] Praise the LORD, O my soul. O LORD my God, you are very great; you are clothed with splendor and majesty. Psalm 104:1 NIV

My work is for my own benefit, yet I stand as an offering to the Almighty who made me His own witness. The benefit of my own unity to God is to align to His way of thinking so I am not alone in my efforts to reach others. I have the value of God and in the manner of knowing Him I shall offer insight based on Scripture. Leading is not the only way to achieve the way ahead for the best influence of knowing where to align is found in the offered role of God to me. I have the knowing aptitude of a gifted individual who has the goal of being tied to care for a life of hope and beauty. To know the prosperity of sharing hope is to have the support of the Most High within me. The value of God is not simplistic nor is it a value of only work efforts. I am not one to ascertain where man is faith bearing but I learn and develop a way forward due to the work of God in me. I have the idea I am not the one to be standing in the manner of support as I am merely a human not the one of unity. God is the way to prosper so invest in His wise counsel to affirm where to lead and how to offer the true knowledge of His caregiving. I shall not lose my witness for I am ever righteous and true due to the work of God in me. I have the same goal as God. To lead and to offer hope so others find the way to live in harmony to the One of hope. I have the work of God in my idea making so I build in support of His lead.

Leading is the plan for man to gain and inherit the value of good standing in where the future holds a value. I have not witnessed anything greater than the Risen I AM who holds the hope for man in Him. The lead of sharing the right birth is to call on the One who ordained you to know Him. The intent of God is for all to lean into the way of His caregiving. I now have the work of God growing in my body and it stands to reason I have a purpose in this venture. No other way has been put in motion where all of mankind prospers. I do not have the knowledge of what is to come but I now see a better path coming. To know the way of faith is a guide in where many find the light as a gifted witness. The plan of the Mighty Warrior is to place man on the pattern of growing insight, so others claim Him for their own livelihood. I aim for the suturing of the goal to be one of support not loss. Do you yourself hear the voice of the One who made you? In the manner of sharing the offer you witness to mankind God is who He professes to be. If you place your heart in His hand, you have the intent of knowing Him with pleasure in abundance. The perfect way He manages is for all to share in the wealth of Him. He never rejects a person based on his own unity but rather when He is embraced, He calls man to Him with inspiring faith. I am tying my own dream state to the One of insight. I have the work of God in me, and I witness due to the hope I found. He is ever faithful to me, and I gain in the way of sharing His way. The love of God captures the one who places value to Him not his own manner. God supports the unity, and the growth is a balance of favor and aptitude. Leading is not for the one who has not given his incentive to a need. It takes time to gain in the way of shared hope. The role of man is to align to the Gateway and push forth into Him with support. God is perfect and does not have any faults. He alone is the plan of hope for He is the gift one needs to gain by. I know I am tying my spirit to Him with hope and in doing this activity I lean into Him in favor. The bond is one of cement not a false flag of doubt. Knowing the way to act leads me in a steady goal making process. I have the incentive to prepare much for the sake of those in need. I shall not lose my inherit gift of insight as the true nature of God is within my heart.

The role of my knowing where to apply and how to perform is not my own undertaking. I have been given the voice of God to me in a personal way. I hear Him speak and I look at what He determines for me to be as. The work of my stand is to be as He is where able. Knowing the value of God is far greater than all I have seen in all my witnessing. He is the stand of holy gain not I. I value Him as my mentor, and I feel attached to Him in support. I learn by His counsel and in His value system I am fed support. Do I need more constructive goals? God alone is the way to learn and have prosperity.

In Him is the unity I have been given. I look to Him for my advancement, so I enter in the plan of truth. To believe in the God of man is to tie my influence on His person, not an indifference in no future. I evaluate the love I have been given, and I know I am not without a hue of no learning for God has given me the support of His counsel. Reading Scripture is for all to learn from. It is the stand of holy marriage for the person willing to offer insight to himself. Leading is for the man who places value to the ones beneath his knowledge. God is the beacon to my heart. I offer it to others in need. I align to Him in the way of knowing He is my gifted sponsor. I have the unity needed to share His way of being. I gained from His person, and I invite Him to me. Will I know Him on death? I believe this to be the case. I have the hope of Him in me and in this I am given the work of His care. I look to Him for the very breath I take in. His shoulder effect is for man to have the gift of Him as his own. I know I am one of many who plaes value to Him. I divide the Word correctly to develop the path of holy witnessing. Should I ever refrain from sharing the truth of God to man? Not if I lean into Him for the necessary goal making. He is the directive I engage with. I invite Him to me, so I never feel alone or without support. Even now in this era of growing I am given the support to witness I am with His Child. Not by physical unity of the flesh but of a spirit filling. Would I have given this to another? No, I was offered the lead, and I invited the hope to me. God is my main source of freedom and in Him I am the work of His labor. He is the one I offer my heart toward. In knowing Him I am tying myself to His counsel for the purpose of being His committed ally.

My hope is for the man who hears me not my reputation of being the gift but of my Savior being the light and hope of mankind. I have a knowing way of shared insight not of my own value but of the King. He claimed me to know Him, and I have not forgotten who He is to me. My heart embraces the love and care of God and in the way of work I have the Word to lead my thought process. It has been a time of prayer and unity for me to align to God with support. It came where most men are not tying to God for, they feel He is not the gift but they themselves are. The unity I have will not fall into the dust of the day as it carries me into the heart of life. God is my hope and in Him I am given the support to keep pressing into others. Would there be a better formula than this to strive toward? No, for God created the plan and it is right and true. The suggestion is not one of no pondering but to remain on this avenue of ideas is false and not worthy of my efforts. I realize at times I differ from my own value system and that simply supports my knowledge I need the Caretaker to right my movements in time. Are there many who fail and forget who made them? Unfortunately, it does play a role in life but to share the Biblical practices of the Most High is a solid unity none can compare to. I have the heart of a warrior and in the gain, I learn and invest so others also find the gate to freedom. It means to believe wholeheartedly in the saving power of Christ. He alone is the mainframe for man to have a stand of hope not failure. It is by Him I endure and grow with support. He is the value I need to gift others the idea of wealth not of monetary but rather heartstrings of good harmony toward the King. It has taken time for me to see the light in a more positive way. Reading the Book of the Caregiver has meant I am not in the way of no knowledge. I am tying my inheritance to the work of God and finding where I need to live with faith. Man believes he needn't walk in a righteous way until the time of death is near. This is not true nor is it the way to prosper. Knowing the saving power of God in the duration of a life span is the witness guaranteeing the hope of eternal insight. The value of the one who defines the precious love of God is a sight all need to flourish. God is the one who developed the way ahead toward prosperity. It is not tied to cash flow nor is it without a wage of the spirit. In the way of God is the formula to bind to others so man can have the work of God flowing forth to the heart.

The support from God is a sight I engage forward to have. The benefit is of knowing where to step and when to act. I now reside with care as a result, and the glory of God I carry within me. God supported my favor with His person. In the knowledge of Christ, I aim to bear truth forward. This is due to Scripture reading and finding the love of God to be holy and right. I embrace this gift, and I lean into it for livelihood benefits. Leading is not a singular triumph. It takes a lot to make a dream prosper. The work of God is for any who deem Him worth their time and their efforts. I know for me I shall stay connected to the great I Am. He is my all in all. Would it not benefit anyone to learn how to have a life of good intent without harm being part of the equation? God does not strike the man who offers himself in a loving and kind witness. The support from God is crucial to mankind whether he is a believer or not. God aims to benefit all. Yet, there come times where God must discipline the negative with actions that bring into play a correction. Will all who have this happen find God in the mixture of it? Not all choose wisely, and they prefer a life in the darkness. Why does this happen? Only man himself can offer this knowledge for to me it makes no hope build. I lack the incentive to find the answer as it may jeopardize my intake of hope. I value God more than the knowing dark thoughts so there is no benefit to me to study why a person refuses to love the Lord. It takes one the responsive hold to perform in the way of sharing in the heart. Some fear this where I do not. God is the one who created me in His image. To me this is a stand of light I embrace. If I merely thought of another man, it would not be as valued. Learning of where faith resides is what I loved and held fast to. My support is from on high. In the manner of this I aim to build for man to know the God I engage with. It is not a simplistic idea, yet, anyone can achieve this plan. Look at where your insight has been granted. Are there intentions leading to more than self or cash flow? Where is the role of leadership if not from the power of a righteous Being? Let the work of God move within you and find the goal being a bright dream of insight. No loss of value will enter you for God is good all the way through. Dine on His care and find the light of Him leading you to a better thought pattern. You will rejoice in Him and be standing on solid hope with good goals.

My offering of insight came by way of knowing the Word of Christ. I am here due to the influence of hearing it with an open heart. My unity is tying me to God and in Him I am fed support. The glorified lead of Him is for me to align to His caregiving so I learn how to work with clear mindedness. I enjoy perceiving being His offered person of hope, but I merely lean forth in it with no fame or recognized power. He alone is the Gateway to life, and I am here to say He is good. Eternity does not hold people who achieved high standards but rather the hope of God is within them. I too am not the influence of the Great Waymaker. I shall not be the way for life to be glorified for I alone do not offer this plan. I am not one to boast of my gift for any other woman could have been the witness had God chosen her to be so. I offer my body to the caring of the Child of hope and in the manner of being tied to Him I shall offer the learning I have been gifted. I work to trim expressing those who believe I am more than just flesh with spirit within her. God is the Gateway, and I offer this truth to all who place their ears within earshot of my words. I will esteem to share the bounty of God and how He offers light to me with the reward of being His mother in the human form. Is there another who claims God is not the great Being of all? I know man believes he is more than just a person of the Creator's handiwork. But the one who realizes God is the mighty One of all is far more knowledgeable than the one who professes to be great. Knowing where to offer the knowing aptitude is to witness with clear knowledge found in the Book of Hope. The Scripture I learn feeds me the gain and in it is the way to life eternal. God is the Gateway and in Him is the stand of knowing I am not the worker of all things right and true. Will I learn where to find the favor all hope to have? I already have this knowledge for God granted me the work of sharing Him in a righteous way.

The time I invest is a sure gamble as God cares for me like a Father in love with His daughter. I work to give man the knowing gain I acquired. Yet I am not the way to claim it. I value my offering, but I am not the way to life in heaven's household. Work is something all must apply and in doing this act good support is provided. I am not the reward for God alone is this being. The lead of knowing who the right gift is and who is not, comes when the work of a person is given to God. Where the knowing offers their wisdom, a plan of recognition happens where faith is seen, and rewards are granted. The unity of sharing in a proper atonement is for God to set in motion not I. For I have the claim of the One who made me as His offered lead in the testament of faith due to knowing where and how He operates. Should I invite another to do the work God has given me? Where would this align to Him in faith? I have a profusion of favor and in the way of knowing who the desired witness is and who is merely a stand-alone, I have the gift to give others the hope I know. It is not a bragging position I offer but one of faith built on the practice of reading in support of Christ. The Scriptures hold value to my heart, and I place love toward the reading of them. To allow God to work in me with care is an easy stand to support. He is my all in all and I tie to Him in care. I have seen life give me harsh alternatives and I do not relish being outside of Christ. There is no better source of wealth then God and His true nature. I believe I will one day see the benefit of this circumstance, and I align to the claim I will inherit life eternal. It is for me to be standing with character and not of a false idea. I know I am not without pause or concern for all mankind has such thoughts. I look to God for a stand in outreach and I value Him as my own Father and support beam. If I fail it is not due to Him for, I need training daily. God works with the knowledge of the future, so He never makes a mistake in timing or output. I have the faith of knowing He aims to place me with unity, so I never have to offer a harmful intent. Working with God is a goal I express to those who place value to His way of being.

[11] For I know the plans I have for you, "declares the LORD, "plans to prosper you and not to harm you, plans to give you hope and a future. Jeremiah 29:11 NIV

My unity is not a goal of no insight; yet I am tying my heart to the way of the Savior for He is more to me than self-ideas or false instinct. If I knew I would be chosen for this time where would the element of faith be found? I would have had to explain what I knew in advance, and none would place value to God. He is the one who led me to care for His Word and His idea making. In the plan I witnessed the knowing aptitude God is supportive of me in the most profound way. I have the work of man, and I still enjoy being tied to his support, but God alone is my advancement. I knew I would need the voice of reason to guide my endurance and my counseling. I have the will of God in me, so I now realize I am His very spirit being of growth. Leading is significant even if I do it in the way others have before me. To know where to invite Christ to the way of those I meet is not something I take lightly. I am not without a loss due to my own understanding; yet I know I am doing a just plan. There resides the bounty in me, and I invite more of God to me. The distance I share with Him is my own draw for if I advance in His spiritual draw I tie to Him with care. Leading comes to me from on high. The work of knowing where to align is not a simple gesture nor is it a false lead. I am ever growing up with support as I love my Savior and His gift of hope. I am not the unity, but I hold to it for the value of love it presents. I share the work of

God and in the manner of it I am ever filled with hope. Does it mean I do not have moments of loss in the spirit? I am like any other so there are at times less than opportune ways of expressing myself. I remember God is the great One of rich leading and I tie my heart to Him for support. He never fails to adjust my intent, so I am given favor in His way of thinking. He is the reason I live and offer to others a path of hope.

My hearing is of a wise individual who knows the recognized way of favor. Where the Lord carries me is in the progress of sharing light. What would the value be if only I knew the One of hope? To offer my heart and guide the one who follows me is to share the Scripture of insight. Leading is for the one who offers his heart to God and who focuses on His manner not of self-leading. I am tying my faith to the One of gain not my own abilities. I am here due to the love of my Caregiver. He alone supported me with purpose. In Him I am ever generously given hope which makes for my idea making to thrive. Are there implications I need to learn more of the Guide material? All of mankind must continue to acclaim the bounty to benefit and grow in the spirit. I am not the way to know all there is to life. I merely invite God to me, and He adjusts my perspective where I aim to place Him as my guidance Counselor. Sharing the gift of knowing who the Gateway is stands as a solid unity I have been gifted. To offer it to those less fortunate is my goal in Him. I am not the singular reason for faith. That is God not I. In Him is the role of knowing hope in an abundant way. How do I acclaim this is worth knowing? I am witness to the good way of life due to it. I am standing with courage, and I work to guide where faith is placed on the King. God alone is the way to life eternal. Should this matter to mankind? I place value on man but not of such high esteem I cannot recognize man is weak without purpose until God declares a path for him. To follow the Risen God is to place value toward His way of being. How this will come to be I do not understand but the Scriptures say it clearly will happen.

[20] He protects all his bones, not one of them will be broken. [21] Evil will slay the wicked: the foes of the righteous will be condemned. [22] The LORD redeems his servants; no one will be condemned who takes refuge in him. Psalm 35:20-22 NIV

The work of my heart stands as a reward in where I can claim God is my all in all. I have built the way ahead due to study and insight from reading. When God is at work clearing the mind of fog great wealth builds within. Will I never make a mistake in how I operate? Only God alone has the answer to this question. I now see where I tied my spirit to God for a purpose of hope to be given. I am not the singular way to thrive for only God is this witness. The unity and the support are far above anything man can provide so I place my goals in His hands. Where the riverbed is seen fish swim and move about; yet, without a net there is no reward of food supplement. In the same way man must offer what he learns to those who need insight. It can be a simple thing, yet, it will mean a great deal to someone who has not gained the witness you obtained. I have the value of the righteous Leader and in Him is the hope I gained. It comes from on high not my own determination. Little is seen without effort, so I apply my heart to the Scriptures, and I stand on the promises they provide. God supports me in the way of offering me a goal of importance. The leverage I hold is not of power in the muscular way but of the Biblical stand I am redeemed. Did I earn it? No, because I am not good enough to do so. God is the way to have prosperity. He is the offered reward, and I align to Him in the way of a spiritual bond not just head knowledge. He has shown me favor and I have the gift of knowing who He is, and how He operates. With this knowledge I entrust Him with my life. All the necessary leading is not as fulfilling as the way I heard my Savior lead me. God is perfect and right. In Him is the calling of faith not just a voice of no input. He offers my heart the work of His hands, so I align to Him in care. We are tied and in Him I have faith in committing to Him with true honor.

My yearning is from the One of hope. In His value system I have faith to establish more intent leading to others hearing the plan of salvation. How this happens is for God to determine not me. Yet, in this idea I know I am complete. Where is the offered role I see among me? If it is not within man to find prosperity, where does he get the knowledge to thrive? What sets him on the pathway to offer a unity so another will find the necessary favor I have been given? To love the One who made me His is to offer Him my whole being. Would there be another way more prospering, yet, without a loss to some in one form or another? By the witness of care, I have the knowing support God is my lead. He is the offered role of insight I have been given leading to a plan of insight. How do I know this is true? I have the inspiration of the mainstay of support with no harsh ideas or evil intent. God works so I deem Him worthy of my time and unity. He is the Gateway I need to have to be given the life of a supporter. Where would I ever have the reward, I have had if not for evaluating the One of inspiring unity? He captured me as His own and I am persuaded to achieve so I know who the giver of hope is to be. My Child shall offer the world the plan of integrity no one can compare with. Does this bring into view no other is valued where light shines? We are to offer our hearts to the way of hope not darkness. God is the reason I stand in the path of support. He is the way for prosperity to be had. Do I love being in the position of bearing a child outside of marriage? It is not for me to judge but as a woman of today I know I could be stoned for it. God will lead me in this field of time, so I am tied to Him in care. No, I will not completely feel availed, but I am standing here in good health with no one attacking my station. It has been a time of trying influence and some violated my person with comments of harm. Will this make me more of a mature caregiver? I shall have to invest in God to learn of this idea.

Many are the ones who place value to the Risen One of hope. I am yet to hear of His lead for He is not birthed by me yet. But I know I will have the work of His nature to see and incorporate into others. The unity of His way is for all who have the benefit of sharing the gift of support found in Him. I know I tie to His way of thinking as I have the gift of unity to Him. Even though He is not alive outside of my body I know He still hears my call to Him. How do I know this to be? Man hears the voice of God with the unity of Him waiting for a connection to be born. I know it takes the work of a person to lead with caregiving and in the way of it one must bind to the perception God is a goal of faith. I know I am tying my own value to God but in the manner of sharing Him I offer His counsel. The way to thrive is to be vested with support and to guide the heart in the direction of His care. I will not lose my hope if I work with the support of God to me with care building as the stand I lean toward. The leader of man is the One who planned his birthright. God is the reason man exists and in His way is the offered hope to build with care. I know I am not the one who has no value as I am made in His image and in Him is my favor. I work to offer others the respect I have gained and in the growing I am fed insight. What is the plan of God if not to value His creation? Knowing God means to align to His way of thinking. I shelter the knowledge I get, and I offer it forward with hope placing the insight into motion. Where did I gain this hope? God offered it to me in the way of a spiritual bond with the growth of it being of a whole complete unity. I may lose my way at times, but I do not aim to do so. I am offering a project yet to be completed. I know I have the goal of a person who witnesses the knowing way to align in the way of hope and in the gain is the understanding God is the perfect Being of sight. Why does this matter? I would not speak to others if it were not so. I gain where I let God work in me. It takes the hearing of His counsel to build my honor and my support. I now remain in committing a knowing support measure and in this arena, I am given a bounty of insight. How does this happen if not for God's care to me? Man has the idea he can make a thing of beauty by simply offering his knowledge forth to another. What determines whether this is a stand of hope is based on the value found to it. Man can think he knows best when in reality he is a slim understanding of inspiration in where God is the maker of all things right and true. I evaluate what matters to me and I look to that as my instructive lead. Never do I say I am all there is to an answer of some knowledge for God alone is this Being. Unity is for man to know God not for God to learn by way of man's offered thought process.

Glory to God is for the gift of support to be written in the way of faith. Where the knowing has the lead is found by way of support to the heart not the insecure lead of no insight. God values the one who places his heart in the palm of His hand. I work with unity, so I am not without the idea of where I am to tread. Knowing the work is of faith I offer it to those willing to engage with favor. Not all people place their hearts and minds in the way of faith to God. Men find their own way of operating to be self-sufficient; yet, with God there is a better method. To know where to align is to pray and seek God above that of the lead of mankind. Where the faith lives, God carries out the lead and offers the instruction, so bounty thrives, and glory comes forth. To know the way to act is not always a simplistic understanding.

One must stand in the path of knowledge and let God show where He chooses to invest. It may be that no support offered for a period of growth may be happening outside of the area you reside. It takes patience and hope for man to align to the call of support God projected. Knowing the offered role of God is to place your instructed idea on the mission field of design making in where the door to walk through is made abundantly clear. I have the work of my own heart, but I know to offer my goal to God is to acclaim forward to His person. I am not the reason one gifts another his hope, but I do understand where to apply it. God is the one who makes me inspired so I wait on His alignment to gift it toward those in need. I work with care, and I grant my knowledge to any who place value to God. It takes time to see what it is to be and in the manner of it growing forward it is a step to be witnessed with opportunity at the heart of it. I have the will to grant another the faith I have within but without God's instruction I do not know where this is to be.

My influence is small and not complete, but I am tied to the Gateway of life. I know I am not the way to thrive, and I have no offering other than what God provides. It is leadership I claim from on high not of my own merit. I know I have the reward of sharing the gift of support, so others also learn as I have. The unity I share is far greater than that of no hope for man is not who I desire to ascertain from. God is the majestic Being who plans my future and teaches me where to align. In the way of knowing who the skilled One of all comes the ability to offer it to another. Where the lead of God supports me is the hope I must suggest to another where to find the love and inspiring gift I learned. Do all the people I encounter have the hope I lead them to? No, for some do not believe in the God I know. It is a sad thing to witness, and I offer prayers on their behalf. Would not the individual who claims to know more than God not see his own less than aptitude? No thoughts of holiness come to him though and there is no guiding influence of insight. Only by way of God is there an exclamation of unity for He is the spirit Being of knowledge. I am tying my heart to Him in a sound manner so as never to lose His presence in my life. I have the favor of Him, and it is glorious to recognize. In Him is the leading I need to see and know the support of. If no other can stand as God can why is man so harsh against

Him? I cannot unite to the one who places no inspired bounty to God. The hope and the support far outweigh any other ingested gift. God is the one I learn from and in Him is the value I need to acclaim Him righteous and true. The reward of His call is so intimate I hear it with insight not my ears themselves. He supports my goal making and He operates where I need Him most. No reward is giving to me in an economical way concerning the spirit not wealth of the pocketbook. Should I ever lose my way I fear I would be as a fool with no value to man; yet God would love me still. He captures the work of my labor and brings it to the heart as a complete unity where all we witness stands upright. I know I have the knowledge God can ordain to me the pattern of faith, so I act with caregiving as He does. He is perfect and stands in a righteous way, never failing or losing steps. Should I not try to witness as He does? It takes training and value to His person in where I need to achieve the reading of His Word. I know I am not a witness of no support for He offers me ideas and suggestive thought processes where I team with courage and align to His way of thinking.

The love and care of God is far greater than the notoriety of self-expression. I have the goal of giving to man the idea of who God is to me; yet I am not without faults. I am merely a person with a unity that feeds her with support. To know this is to remind one I have the work of God in me, but I am not He. I aim to perfect my unity, but it will not lay claim to this until I passed forth into the heavens above. I shoulder the burden of no insight in where the future is not known to me. God alone is the Gateway to life, and He masters even this knowledge. I have the bonus of realizing I am tying to the way forward in care. Why would it matter to me to offer others my intellect? To know the God of all things right is to claim Him as the Creator of good intent. If one participates in the way of faith, he finds the pathway to learned witness making. It comes to the heart of the one who has the support of Christ within him. I have the work of God and in His counsel, I find unity that is full and true. Where am I leading if not for another to have this viewpoint. It has taken man time to accept God is the way for all to learn and find prosperity. All the generations have had the opportunity to embellish forth the support tying men to Christ with pure objectives. I know it is not a simple gesture to offer another the way to claim God. It takes courage and mastering of the mind to express the light and build it to others. I have the reward of knowing who made me and how He works. I aim to carry forward the work of God and to witness where I am able. The option is a solid way of thinking and in its offering, man finds hope. God supports me in the way of faith, so I can continue to bend to the call of Him. He invites me to align to His care and in doing this action I am fed unity to His spirit.

²³ *I do all this for the sake of the Gospel, that I may share in its blessing. 1 Corinthians 9:23 NIV*

My courage is from the One who made me His own. With His perfect ability I tie to His counsel and align to Him with support. Why does it matter to me to do this action when all I need is to believe and support His way of life? I share the reward of knowing He is the great One of unity. In Him is the reward of faith one must have to grow in a spiritual way. The necessary bounty is not found in knowing how to perform so a plan of gain can be had where money is the favored idea. I now realize it takes more than just a simple goal to have the proper faith of a mustard seed. In the way of doing business, man is tying his manner to that of his own value system. God is the hope man needs having for a better investment to his person. Without the prosperity of God there is no hope for man. Monetary living is not what is the gift of life but rather of the Creator Himself who preserves the spirit and supports the work of the heart. I witnessed the many who place value to the dollar and find it lacking. They strive even more for more intake where only coins come into their hands. I know I need money to survive as does all mankind; yet I am not offering this as my unity to God. He is the way to life eternal and in Him is more than revenue from the pocketbook. His stand is the spiritual connection of sight in where the fruit of the heart is far greater than the offered favor of self-glory or money holdings. I know man needs to pay his way in life but to only allow for riches to be the factor you rush to contribute means there is no true lean of faith within you. Money is not the only idol people succumb to. There are many things men place above the King. It can be a simple thing not accepted as righteous to others who have the support of God, it represents to the man himself a loss. In knowing a certain retention of loss happens one is then in the way of being deceived.

The gift of sharing the light of Him is found in the favor of His counsel. To know God is all care and no indifference is to see Him with unity and love. I am not the birthing agenda. I am the way of uniting to God simply due to the witness I give. I have the work of God and in Him is my value system. I tie to Scripture to gain the insight needed to offer others the way of livelihood. Does this act as the support needed for man to align to God? No, I am not the glue that adheres to the process. I work so others have the knowledge I have been given and in the way of this I gain as well. Sharing the value of Christ is far more valuable than being one who does not invest in Him. The love of God is far-reaching, and it holds value in where man is tying his heart to the Gateway of hope. Know I do not offer this ability, but I guide man to hear the truth of it. I have no gift other than the average human. We all have talent and build with it in forms of light. The reward is a stand in where I have the idea of faith, and I work as though it is in me. I know no other who can relate the worth of a person to his being in such a way only goodness is given. The man who believes he needs something other than God is a person who has not claimed God for himself. To stay on the outside of care is a false directive denying the power of God and His presence to man. I have the choice of knowing where to gift the light and in doing this act I guide so another is given support. It blesses me to do so, and I find it favoring to me in a personal way. God atones the spirit, and He gifts the heart the path forward. To know the way to offer the lead of significant idea making is to align to God and prepare the path for another to invest in turn feeding the upright goal to others. In the value of a goal comes the where withal to align to God or step outside of His way. If one places value to Him good harmony is maintained. Offer your knowledge to the one who needs to see a way ahead and find the growth a bounty you can acclaim forward. In the negative work no hope is granted so what point is there in life? Work should carry forth to the one who knows how to operate in the sight of caregiving. With it is the moral lead offering the unity found from on high. Many learn a talent and are not willing to offer the way it came to be due to the threat of no recognition to them personally. When knowledge is captured in the process of education growth will maintain the heart and beauty will bloom.

Christ is the one who made me His caregiver for this time. I am to be the one to mother the Child of Unity. Why was I chosen, if not to be a witness to His moral righteousness? I have the learning of an individual who knows how to handle the written Word. I apply it to the plan of my life, so I inherit the work of it to me. I know there is little left to undertake where I offer others knowledge; yet I am claiming it forth to all. Is the abundance a fulfilled work of God? I believe there is more to be delivered. I aim to adjust my focal point to God who hears my unity to Him. I have the will to align to the One of Great Hope, so I never lose my footing or act out of self-preservation. Knowing God carries me with His person to a height in where I am tied to Him in a structured way. He alone is the One I admire. He offers me the pathway to thrive, so I know how to have an abundance of love. The goal of God is for man to know Him in a personal way. How this comes to be is reading the Word of His counsel and praying to Him in faith. I am not the weak bodied person who has no influence on God. He has given me a source of hope no one can compare to. Why would I ever leave the comfort of God for the sake of no offered gain? There is no point in doing this. Leading is the way to offer others the value of God for the advancement to His manner. I have known the support of God's care, and I find it filled with hope. I claim to have the written Word within me, and I now realize it matters to me to be standing in its wave of light. The Word is not slim in nature for there is more within it than simply writings. The work is complete and right. The way to thrive is to align to the One who planned for you to live. He alone benefits the heart and in Him is the gateway to eternal witnessing. The look of faith is plentiful and the ability to know where to offer this input is steadfast and true. Love is the main purpose to turn to God for it is ever present where He resides.

My unity is not one of no bearing for the Word teaches me I am cared for. I have a knowing way to perform so others find me favoring to their minds. I believe I have the gift of prophecy to teach and to lead so others hear who to have faith toward. I do not know the future nor will I for God has spoken to me only of who to have faith in. The Word is my incentive to flourish and strive to. I am not the Gateway that will be the One I carry within me. I will lead Him with knowing a person who found faith in Scripture not my own understanding. To value the work and care of God is to align to Him with support. Sharing the right way to act is a solid draw in where man is tied to God with character. The work of me is to lean forward and provide the value of God to others. Why would I ever look for another plan when the Word provides the answer to the way of life. The Word is the all-encompassed value I need to learn by. I share due to the will of my God supporting me to do so. He is the One who offers to me the plan of salvation. How this will happen is not known at this time, but my influence is not the gift, nor will it be. I simply witnessed what I know, and I learned the true nature of the Almighty. The Word provided me with unity. And in the way of it I am tying my goal making to the Gateway in where I aspire to learn and develop the true nature of God to my heart. The Word provides me with insight and in the way of knowing where to align I find support. Will I lose my way if I do not continue to perform for God as I have been? It is not the effort that enables me to gift my heart the Word. It is the call of God to me in the way of preventative measures that secures me to Him. I learn to operate so I have the insight of His counsel. I believe I am not worthy to gift someone the knowledge, but I have the support from God to be made in the image of Him. This supports me to witness for His namesake. Unity is solid, and the performance is of a true means of hope. Knowing where to land when problems are in the mix is a support I learned from on high. Accepting life has its ups and downs is the unity all need to perform so there resides the love and support of God to their instructed hope. Knowing the support is from God is what means the hope is real. Leading is for the man who hears the Word and applies it to his intake of value. Knowing I have the support of the superior Being is a solid idea I am in support of.

God almighty is always willing to invest in the one who looks to Him for the idea of how to operate with support to another in need. I have known the Word and in it I found the unity necessary to align to God's caregiving. This is the notion to man to offer others the work we impose to living in a free manner. The goal to align to God is a solid way to claim Him as holy. I have the work of my own hands in where I am tying the resolve of my heart to the lead of Christ. Will I know Him by His witness to me after He is born? I believe there will be a definite difference between He and I. I am mere flesh, and He is spiritual. His assembly may look like man but within Him will reside a very different way of being. I know I have the knowledge God cares for man. It came to me from a scholar who taught me the truth of Scripture. The plan of the One of Hope is for all to know Him in a personal way. Why this makes a difference is due to the love value God has for His people. The way to unify Him is prayer and support in His way of being. The light of Him is for any who believes and finds Him favoring. Holiness is not something to lose the value of. In His creativeness we were formed. The unity to His offered care is righteous and true. When one places his heart in the palm of God's caregiving, goodness is given. Learning where to align to His calling is a solid gift in the way of shared cooperation. God is the perfect influence and in Him is the support of the heart. I yearn for Him to claim me to Him. I work today as a sired being of His inspiration. I have the hope of Him within me. I evaluate where he leads, and I work for the glory of Him to be shared. Knowing He is generous and true is a plan in where I now claim Him as my only presence of faith. He alone is the Gateway to live and to advance in a suturing of honor. His standard for man is not slim in the way of favor. He gives man the way to align to His care in a simplistic way. There is no price tag applied but one must believe and invite Him to him. I alone can decide for my own self whom I shall invest in. It takes time to learn where God desires for you to gain in His value system. Not all have the same invested skill set as another. To know where to gift the outreach is found by experience and knowledge. I know I am tying to the way of God where I offer my own intake to Him. The love of His counsel speaks to me with unity. The witness of Him is solid and true. The way of support feeds me with a bonded growth no one can compare with. Should I ever face hardship I will have the faith in Him to lean on. He stands as my guide, so I know I am in good hands with His support being ever present for me to gain by.

No one is alone if they pursue the Savior with their whole heart. God made Himself available so all can know Him with unity. Have you embraced God, or do you not feel as though you have a need? This is the difference between someone willing to learn and one who did not vest to gain truth. The work of the Lord is a call from on high. Leading is not on a whim from the Master. He is the stand of hope man needs to have the imprint of life on Him. The work of Christ is not a shield with no instructed value. The entire lead is of value of the heart and mind. To physically live without knowing God is a false dream of no value. Only God has the offered hope needed to enter faith with insight being given. I have the work of knowing God cares for me. It is not a secret for I share it freely. I have spoken of it to those near to me and it is good to know I offered the information to them in a free way. The doorway is set apart for the believer. The reward is not a monetary gain but one of knowledge and goal making. If you recognize the support by way of faith you have the claim to God and His manner is within you. Dreams come to the one who places value to Christ. In making a goal bright insight is built. Leading is not on a whim of no value where God does the pulling action. Your heart receives the message but if you reject it a dark impression forms. With each advance in the direction of a dark thought hardness is placed where light could have bloomed. To know the Gateway exists is within all of mankind. There will always be the question as to where God can be heard. He will work in the heart and draw one to Him in the value of His person. Bright ideas come to the one who knows the spiritual leading of God. Unity is found in the prayers and the offered care. God is perfect and just without a loss within Him. The glory of His name is ever before our hearts and minds. To pretend this is not the case is a lie from the pit itself. Be diligent and support the Word of God and know He is value to you in a righteous way.

[16] *All Scripture is God -breathed and is useful for teaching, rebuking, correcting and training in righteousness.* [17] *so that the man of God may be thoroughly equipped for every good work. 2 Timothy 3:16-17 NIV*

Glory to God is not weak or in the manner of no hope. To know the One who made you thrive is to align to His care and be fed by His unity. God is sympathetic to the way of hope not the stand of no intake without the knowledge of His counsel. God is the gift man needs to grow and have an abundant way of life. Work to know the King and stand with support to His way of being. It will mean a better instructed reward and sharing will come with ease. God is true to His nature never diverting to a false way. To know who He is to me has been a hope built with support leading to gain in the spiritual bond. God has the filled idea I am His child and knowing Him has been a unity of insight. To work so another has the gift of God is to see His counsel as trustworthy. God captures me with His goodness. He is ever standing with support to me as I labor to provide in the way of support to my life. He is never without the meaning of good caregiving. I have the work of bonded insight and due to this goal, I am tying others to God. It meant to align to God with hope not just the idea of His good way. The look of God is far greater than the idea He is not real. To understand who claims the King is to realize not all believe as they should. Some prefer to operate with no intake to Him. This means there is little to claim His honor to. If you have the knowing gift of who God is and how He works you have the unity of His person. Stay in the way of knowing this and perform with care so another can see the great way of Christ. Were I not to have seen with my heart I would not have the value to Him I have been provided with. It took me offering my own unity to His person and the gain came immediately. God inspires me daily. He casts the plan of a witness so I can offer it to others who are in need just as I am. I value my own unity to God and without this perfect bond I would flounder.

Robin (Rochel) Arne

Gift Five

Power From On High Has Come to Man

God supports me in the way of sharing His hope to man. He does it so I engage with more than my own inherit lead. I have the value of God and in knowing Him I am made righteous. I look to Him for counsel and insight. The promise of Christ is on every page of Scripture notes. I aim to be an author of knowing work not just one of no insight. I have the reward of sharing Him, so others too gain as I have. The will of God is to be tying man to Him in a personal way. The lead of God is for all to hear where to align and how to live in a just way. I now have the goal of sharing the witness of a tried Being of insight. It comes by way of important knowledge not found outside of God's caring Book. To learn so another has the gift you hold is to allow another the upright stand of support leading to a goal of prosperity. I know I am not the way to thrive for that is God alone; yet I enjoy outreach in where I say to others who is the Waymaker and how to know Him. I have taken the liberty of belief and placed it into the heart of those willing to have my support. I look at who claimed the way of bright leading and find many are still not in the unity measure I witnessed. God is the way to gain and in Him is the offered support one needs to adjust and be abundant in caregiving. I learn by way of a committed bond and in His support beam I am tying love to others. The plan of hope is based on the Word of God and not of my own understanding. It is by the plan of salvation man finds the gift of light necessary to learn and prosper. I lead so others too have the committed hope I arrived at. I am not the lost soul I used to be for God ordained me as His child. I am not the work of no father for God above is this to me. He captured me to Him, and I offer this to man. Where does my hope come from if not from God? How would I learn or know what is true? Is man a teacher in where he never makes mistakes? The lead of the One who knows all there is to life is far greater than the acceptance man has value to one another.

With knowing is the hope and the knowledge of a good witness. I aim to find the hope man needs to learn and be fed unity. I claim it for myself and in the way of it I am never without the love value of God to me. I thank Him for never walking outside of my path and in the manner of Him I am fed light. Expressing sharing the hope is for any who accept God for who He is not the very idea of Him for man has faults when he contemplates all. Where the plan of knowing comes forth man determines the lead, and the honor of God is great.

My voice is not one of hope for I alone am not worthy to be heard. However, with the support from on high I train and learn so when I offer the knowledge of Christ others gain. Where the plan of a witness is given offers of inspiration build. Know there is no other being in where all knowledge flows. Only God Himself is the great Waymaker. In unity to Him we are found with care and opportunity. I know I do not have the ability to align to the great One of hope without the building development of faith. It means I must pray and call on the One of instructed caregiving. I have the work of God and in Him is the value of many. I shield my own care where I embrace the King and align to Him. I have the sight of the mighty God I have come to know and recognize. The unity to God is for all to acclaim a better formula to live by. The vested work is true love and care toward those in need around them. I know I am not the Gateway, nor will I ever be. Only God is this glorious and true. He never loses perspective, nor does He permit another to if they support Him in faith. He builds where He is invited so invest in the way of Him and follow His value system. It will mean a plan will unveil and glory to God will be had. I act as a person who has the work of God within her. I elevate my heart to Him so I can offer it to others who esteem God as righteous and holy. To know the way to thrive yet reject it is foolish and without instruction in where hope resides. I know many have the idea they can act with no value to God and still have life abundant. They merely attest to the fact they have no insight into His person. The unity of knowing how God works is to have within you the governing way of His spirit. The support of the One of who made you is far above that of self-realization. Care needs to be granted for hope to be present. A man who places no value on God only invests in his own way not of the Author of him.

The suggestive way of sharing light is not a symbolic goal but rather a harmonization of the spirit. I know I am not the only one who delivered this proposal to mankind. For generations man has had the opportunity to know God and to hear Him speak. God's focus is for man to have life abundant in where hope resides and the path to life eternal is clear. He alone is the Gateway. No other can claim he has the plan of hope for man is limited in his abilities. I know I am not without faults, but I do try to aspire to be better. I work so another hears the message of preparing light and this means I am tying my heart to the Living Word. I know I am working to grow the offered lead in where I align to God in care. He alone is the way to know peace, and I find it ever rewarding. The value of God is far above that of any other. He is the pathway to know the best option to learn by. I have the gift of sharing Him and I am thankful for it. He has given me the way to read, and, in terms of value, I found Him favoring. To study and to apply to learn the true nature of God is to offer it to the heart and take in the unity. He adores the person who appreciates His way of thinking. I know I am going forth into the open with my thought process, but I do not believe it won't have meaning. I look to the Word for a better hope and in it is the way to live with clear intent. How do I know this is accurate? The reward is within me. I never lean into a false hope where there is no light. It would look like a fake in the spiritual sense. God is perfect and true, and this is the way to have prosperity. God offers the value of Him to me, and I now have the knowing way of His character. It matters to me whom I choose to pursue. Look at who you believe is the way of insight and you will see a path to God. He is ever present to call on and in Him is the goal of knowing how to thrive. The work of God is far more than just a simplistic claim of wealth. The ladder to freedom is in the work of God to the heart. I am not standing on my own instruction here. I read the Book of Insight and found it supports this knowledge. Where is the plan of hope, if not provided by the One who made you?

My instruction has the vault of life within its perimeter. The favor is all encompassed. I know I have the unity to God I hold fast in and the number of men I led to Him is not known. Yet, here I stand in complete awe to God. He is the active way to have favor. It is His unity I aim to be with, not my own undertaking in where there is no real hope. God supports the work of my ministry and in the way of shared goal making me tie as the insight from on high. The Word of God is for all not just me or another. It is the way to thrive and have life eternally tied to Him. I thank His lead in my favor and in the manner of His way I have the appetite of a well-fed individual. In the witness of insight comes the bounty of shared learning. The respect and efforts I have been led to offer tie me directly to His support. I know I am not alone where I have the learned goal of no value for God is the market I attend to. He made in me the unity of a solid person who values His calling above that of her own ideas. In the way of sharing the light is the support needed to adjust the spirit to live in accordance with life and love. The way of a shared bond is not of no value where God is concerned. He is the one who places me in His calling. I hear His way of being and I align to Him due to the love of His support. He is ever faithful and true. In Him is the net worth of a shared spirit. I gained in the prosperity of His counsel. He leads me to the gateway of His favor. In His support is the hope I need to practice the unity of His name. He is spiritual and good. God is my direct line to a nourishing hope. The idea of sharing Him is a solid goal and I evolve in it with caring qualities. He is an earthquake in the making concerning accepting all who come to Him with value to His way of being. I factor in His manner, and I align to Him in a just way. Is there room for improvement? Yes, definitely! I am as all mankind is. Weak with no hope until God speaks to me with just workings. I have the aptitude of shared bounty and in the manner of Him I am tied with concern. I am thankful for His role of leading and I tie to Him with character. I follow Him in a united way due to His counsel and my reading of it. I value Him in all ways that apply to His way, and I thank Him for His favor. I have the gift of knowing where to apply the work of His gifted instruction, so I never fail or feel alone. It takes the spiritual guiding of the great I AM for goodness to be known. Work is not complete if there is no true order to it. In the way of sight, I am given to faith not loss. God has perfect timing, and I plan as though He will be at my side in where I work with good harmony to His way. Should I flounder I know I am not right with His reconning. I love Him and in His forgiving way I tie with the unity I dream of knowing. He alone can bring me into His armor of insight. He calls me to Him, and I thank Him for the instruction. He is the Gateway, and I am the being He loves.

My unity is for all to know and have the accepted value toward. I know I am with God where He operates and how He grants the work of Him forward. I share the hope I gained and in the way of putting it into action I know I am qualified to visualize His goal making. He is the means to life. In Him is undertaking of a significant lead. He creates in me a lifelong hope that multiplies in support. I know I am with His calling when things are right and true. Where He invites me, I stand with His caregiving. He shows me the favor, and I accept it with hope. The faith of my inherit work is not of no insight for God favors me with understanding. I am the one who performs the hands and feet of Him as He has chosen this for mankind. But if He wanted to perform in another fashion He certainly could. I look to Him for the hope I need to continue to maintain my desire to thrive. In Him is the hope I need to align to His calling. At times I must wait for Him to move and show me where I am to act. It means I have accepting of His support within me. I believe God works so I can offer others His support through my offered insight. I have the option of no further attendance with Him but that is not what I choose. I claim my Lord in the way of shared value to Him. He unites my work with others and in the calling I am tied to His way. We are in unity to bend the hearts of man to Him in a personal way. Does He need me to do this? Certainly not! But I am the gift of His work not the one who witnesses to the spirit. God favors the one willing to adjust his thinking to Him. I let God speak to me and to gift me what He values for me to do. At times changes come into play and there is a different viewpoint, but it never is one of a dark impression. There will reside the mirror image of God to me. Hope will be present, and love will also be standing in the mix. I evaluate what is needed and what may work for me to achieve my goals. If there is merit to what I hope to create then I move forward and work with the offering. God knows better than I do as to what is the plan for life, so I let Him feed my objective. I look to the way of God to know what the support from Him is. I invite Him to align to me so I can offer another the work of my heart. In the way of sharing light comes the faith needed to abound in favor. The gift of knowing who is the One of standing is a value none can be compared with. I love God and in Him I am given hope. Does this mean I will always have an abundance of life within me? At times I will have down moments, but they won't bend my spirit into action of no hope or losses. God will perfect my outlook and make me stand with support. He will do this with caregiving, not a dark force of violent math. In His way is hope tying me to His counsel which is solid and forever guiding me in support. I know God has the equation determined so I never have to worry I will not be valued.

My outlook is for me to see more of God rather than less of Him. I can thrive on my own but what would the value to me be? There is simply no better influence of faith than God on high. He captures man and shows him where to align. In Him is the gift of support we need to ascertain where to gift hope. God supports the one who places value to His calling. I heard the gifted way of knowing where to stand and in the way of it I am tying my heart to His care. Would there be another so beneficial to me? Never, for God is the one who performs the best plan to mankind. I have the knowing way of faith within me. It leads me to a better formula and in it I have training in where light is plentiful with caregiving. I work to lead and to gift others the knowing gain I found. It was freely given so there is no price tag tied to it. Simply place your heart in the way of God and find the faith needed to support your intent. God is faithful to offer His way to you. You will hear the better growth and in the manner of sharing Him hope is provided.

My power is slim and with a time value. I cannot be tied to the way of God if I fear when death may take me. I work to offer many the knowing gain of freedom and in it I have complete hope. The work of God is not a material leading. He is spiritual and in Him is the sight plan of faith. To work so many find the intent as good is to place value to God in a spiritual way. He is the one who aligns to the Word and in Him is the factoring of support that gifts the heart a path of unity. To witness the love value is to see where to stand and how to operate so faith is abundant. If you feel depressed or without a goal, stand with God and let Him decipher where to offer you a substantiated goal. I have no knowledge of the intent of God if He does not show me where to plan and where to grow my knowledge. We work with the unity, so I aim to please His purpose for me. I grow with courage when I act on behalf of God not against His value system. My wonder of where to give one gift to another is not something I found disappointing. I invite the work of God's care to my person, and I have the goal of knowing where to gift so others learn as I have. I work with the willing, not the one who acts against me. It has taken time for me to adjust to the care of Christ due to my own influence. My favor from above is a unity I adhere to, and I thank Him for His patience in me. The love value of the Risen I AM is far greater to me than anything else. He is solid and true and in Him is plenty. I work with caregiving, and I lead where I am gifted the hope. I work to achieve, and, in His manner, I align to His calling. It is just where hope remains, so I enact the favor of God to me. I am not a simplistic leader for I have the gift of sharing in a care filled way. Even the slightest intent is seen as true where God is the focal point to the offered stand. I shall never fail if I attend to the faith God provides and, in His support, I will have the unity He portrays. Little is the one who never places faith into action.

Power is for the one who places unity in the hand of the Father. He grows the heart and teaches it a stand of insight. In Him there is the value of knowing where to align and how to portray the hope of His counsel to many. I work in this fashion. My will is to offer the same unity God gifts to me. He shows me where to offer the pattern of faith and how to perform so another hears His voice to him. I am tying my heart to His support. I never feel distracted in where I invest so the heart has the reward to God. It has taken me the learning skill of the written Word to know where to adjust the faith and how to offer it to others. I work when the light of God is within my sight. He is the Gateway I need to see where to land in safe keeping. To know Him is a stand of support, few realize. I aim for the heart of God not His hand of opportunity. Yet, He guides me into a reward system that completes my identity. Knowing the value of God is an idea of more than value to the expectation I need wealth to live. He provides so I have all needed to be well tended to. Do I have every goal met with Him at my side? The value of God is far above the net value of the pocketbook, but He maintains my heart, so I am fed support. I do not lose the idea He can gift me with all necessary measures to survive for that is how He portrays in Scripture. Even the birds of the air have the Word of God providing them favor. He is secure to my love. He ever aligns Himself to my person and the reward is not slim. I have the heart of the One I know as King but to me He shines with value. I expect this Child will know firsthand how to adjust my thinking to His viewpoint. I will not try to dissuade my knowledge for He is far above me. I will teach Him where to find the Word of His counsel so He grows with support as He should. I know He will favor my effort and cause me no harm. To evaluate the true nature of God is to believe He is righteous and true. My endeavor to Him will never change as he is my Caretaker. I work to assist where able, and I know I am not the One who knows all there is to understand. My feedback will not be forgotten but I will not be the great plan of salvation. Any who feel connected to me for the purpose of this is standing in a negative idea. Read the lighted Book and know God is the value not I. Glory to God the Father is what I desire to present. He will never fade away nor will He cause me to wonder where to grow. He worked for my benefit, and I aim to favor Him for all time.

⁴⁶ And Mary said: "my soul glorifies the Lord ⁴⁷ and my spirit rejoices in God my Savior, ⁴⁸ for he has been mindful of the humble state of his servant. From now on all generations will call me blessed, ⁴⁹ for the Mighty One has done great things for me- holy is his name. Luke 1:46-49 NIV

The suture of God to me is a personal benefit I hold dear. My love value to God is not a small witness of no intent. For it takes the heart a commitment of faith to believe and have the stand of support necessary to learn and be given hope. I work so others can abide in the way of unity just as I have been given. I look to the One who made me His own and I have the unity to His calling. The value of God is far above that of another and in Him is my viewpoint of life. He provided me with a true way of support, and I invest in Him with a bonding glue. I am not willing to tarnish my outlook by pretending He is not the all-inspired hope to man. I know I am tying my heart to His spirit and in doing this action I have the unity to His way. I lack no monetary thing and in the way of sharing the light I have followed the true way of Christ. Do I never fail at the witness I give? I am human and not the Gateway for all things bright so I will have a fallen time, but the norm is for me to ascertain the way forward and true. I am given into the wealth of the unity, and it is my hope to align to God in perfect working ways. I intend to act with proper leading, and I will not look to others for my intake of spiritual knowledge. The Book of support is tying me in the way of all-encompassed leading and it is right and good for me to align to its value. I work to adorn my own self, so others find the gift of salvation a thing to gain from. How all this will come to be is for God to perform not I; yet, there is a stand of insight within the page material of the Word.

God carries me to Him in prayer, and I have the work of His counsel in me. Why does this matter to a person? One is not all-knowing as God is and in the way of it none other is as solid in understanding. I have the work of God and in Him is my hope for life-giving support. I know I am tying my goal making to His person and in the goal itself, is the support I need to align to the Gateway who is to come. He will know me by name as His mother but to me He will be my Child. I view this idea as a surprise because I could not have guessed I would be chosen for such a role. Viewing man to my Son will be of a basis of gain. He will have many who call on Him for the faith to complete daily life. I shall not stop from being one who places value to Him in the form of guiding, so He prospers in the Word. I will aim to align to the knowledge of Scripture and in the growth, I will offer the hope I have been granted. To learn where to profess the plan of a witness is a guiding insight due to reading the faith-based Book of light. The way of knowing where to gift it to another comes into view when one dines on extending God's care. I know the way to recommend the favor to man, but it is up to each person to claim God for himself. I work with good intent, so others find the way to God a reward. I know I am not tying man to God merely offering the knowledge of how to find Him. Glory is a gift to God and in the plan of it I say yes to God's idea of living in harmony to Him. I invite my God to me in a fashion of shared goal making. We are not alone, yet we do not see God in His natural state. I view the Savior to come as a beautiful gift to man. He will be the Gateway to live in hope and fruit of the heart will be present. I know not all will pursue the Word as I have so there will be many who have no hope within them, yet they will believe the lie that is present. The difference is only seen in the one who plans for God and his initiative of inspiring light.

The hope of my heart resides in the love of God to me. I know I tie to Him in support which brings Him to me in a calm way. Inviting His spirit is a solid hope I know exists. He is the Gateway to life where I merely exist to honor Him. I love being one of His followers for it matters to me to be one.

I have taken time to evaluate the prospering way of Him, and I find it a reward to know Him in a personal way. The Spirit is of God but the heart at times rejects the hope it provides. I lead with the intent of others learning just as I have how to know God with hope. The offered lead of Christ is of a superior intake and in the manner of His counsel I learn where to be fed. It is never a time of loss for acting with insight leads those around me with clear value. I shall not lose my outlook for I offer it to myself by reading the plan of God. He is the value I need to commit to Him with support. In the bounty is the gain and I have the work of God as proof to me I am with Him in His stand. Leading is not that of no value for man requires a value of support he cannot provide. To look to God and know Him is to accept Him as the support lead one needs to thrive. I have the idea God is good and in the way of sharing the hope I lead with clear insight. God is not the math equation of no inspiring value. He is the plan man needs to learn and invest with care. I shall always have the unity and when I apply my heart to God, I have the gift of Him shining bright in my spirit. It takes the will of the heart and mind for this to happen. I have the idea of knowing where to grow and how to plan so a commitment happens that feeds my suturing to Him. He is the doctor, and I am the patient. He is the all-knowing One of support and in Him is the light for all to gain from. Do I need to see another plan to have reconning? No, for there is no other idea that equates to the fame of God and His ability to teach man how to gain. He is trained well, and He always maintains His heart. He does not invite a lie to Him as He is holy through and through.

My witness is for man to discover who the righteous One of hope truly is. He is all things right and true, yet He never committed a false pretense. How is He so good? No one knows Him that well to answer such a question. I lead in the way of sharing, but He pulls my heartstrings to Him. I evaluate the notion God is perfect but to believe He is more than this is right. I have the hope He will never leave my heart and in the manner of this I act with courage for the Scriptures teach me God is faithful to those who pursue Him in faith. To walk on as though God never existed is to stave off the light and focus on dark ideas. The unity of God to me is far above that of no insight. He has the call to me that supersedes any other draw. In His way of being is the light of integrity all need to give hope to man. Instructing support is found where man reads the Book of light. It is all things required to know God and who He is to man. I love the Word of God, and it completes my heart. All have the plan before them if they choose to follow it with hope. I am not the singular reason God gifts me His honorary self. He loves all people, not just the ones who support Him. I have the will of God within due to offering my instruction to His person. I am not without the loss of having taken time to determine who my Father is. I do not know when it happened but any time away from the God I know is too long. Even as a child of a young age I knew Him, so I assumed I entered His counsel as an infant. Even though I have no recollection of this I stand on the promise of it. I have the idea He is all-knowing, and He could hear my profession to Him even in a silent witness. I do believe I spoke to Him with support whether it was in the infancy stage or toddler God heard me and it was complete. I thank my God for His knowledge. He alone is the carpenter who knows the plan of life for every person on earth. We are not without the hope of Him if we stand for His care and lean into Him in faith. I am not the only one to know this is true. Many followed God and found Him to be supportive of their hope. I learn where I am fed, and this is with God's counsel to me. It is the one thing I can adhere to with certainty. The all-knowing value of God far surpasses my own understanding. I have the goal of knowing Him in a rich way. I apply the truth of God to my heart, and I gain from it. The value of Christ is for me to learn and have support not losses. The very way God works stands as a righteous means not one of no hope. The singular way of God is far greater than any man's dream could ever be. I will work to acclaim Him to another, so they inherit the value of His counsel. Tying to God is far above any other instruction. God will always be my main attraction, and He will support my love to Him. It will mean we are more than one to another but of a stand of hope in where we act together in support giving one another love and true honor.

God's care to me is ever before my heart. I know I am tying to Him in care. He lifted my own understanding to include that of His might. He is far above man and in this I realize I have much to learn and give to others. I value the law of God, and I know there will be another whose heart is tying man to

Him. He will be the Gateway to life in abundance. I have Him within my womb, but I know I am just as any other who needs her Savior. I am trained to perceive the value of God and in doing this action I am revealed as a valuable member of God's people. I look to God for the actual realization of where I am to be planted but for now, I live in the region of Bethlehem. It is not a well-known area but one day it shall be recorded for another to learn because this is where the Messiah will be living. It will be a place of worship in that many will team with another to visualize the whereabouts of God. For it is written man will know the region of His God's birth. I do not believe I must develop in some form outside of the witness the Savior has shown me. I evaluate the true nature of God, and I invite Him to me to tabulate where the entry of hope begins to be recognized. I know there will be those who do not believe in the promise and who stand aloof in the way of no support. They will lose the love of God and have no hope for the future. If one places support to the Waymaker a life of good value will engulf them. It may not be until they are captured up into the heaven's orbit but nonetheless it will happen. I am with the people who place their hearts in directing God and His favor. By being in unity with Him I have the idea I can make a difference in the way of supporting Him with love. He does not forsake me nor will He ever. I have an abundant way of being in that to know God is to call Him my favored light. He is the way to thrive and learn hope. Even if none ever come with me in the growth, I will still stand on the lighted way of God to me. He is valuable and in Him is my offered unity. If I am to say it is a gain, I must know Him to be able to do this. Reading is sufficient and it teaches me where to align to God. I will not lose the heart of the warrior I now embrace for it matters to me to gift man the knowing bridge of God to his own understanding. Light is for any who place value in directing care and hope. With unity I gain in the manner of knowledge supportive to life in the wealth arena. This is what makes it all worthwhile to know the God of all.

The many who have fallen are not going to inherit the value of God due to their own witness against them. If no support to God is given in your stand why would God carry you to the heart of Him? He would rather you have the gift you choose than force Himself on you even though His way means life eternal where hope resides forevermore. Little daily practices can build the heart toward the One who places His heart on mankind. It means to allow God the ability to perform within you a lighted pathway, so you learn and gain His manner. Do you enter a room where you are not welcomed? No, man does not lean into those who step outside of his heart. To know the One of intent is to offer your inherit learning to Him in support and love. I have the gift of salvation due to accepting the light God provides. Will it change once my Child is born? I do not have the answer to this question, but I know greatness will be had. Many are now leading in the way of no faith, and they are merely saying light without it being tied to God and His way. The difference is the offering is not secure, nor will it be all consuming of the heart. Where God is given the work of Him to another goodness is built and the reward is given. People today say they don't need to know Scripture for it matters to no other to learn it. Such a false claim that is! Knowing the value of God is what preserves the spirit and guides it with support. I now say with certainty there is no other thing outside of Christ that can witness as pure and holy as He is able to. I aim to be one of His people in that speaking to others for the gain of them having God as their Savior is to define the hope and put it in motion. The value of God is far more than silver or gold in that the richness is ever forthright. To evolve with care and apply it to others is to stand on the inherit worth of God not the holding of deception. God is ever giving to the one who prefers His way than that of the negative. The repeat offender realizes he needs to be forgiven on a regular basis. With God the claim to be washed in the blood means salvation in the way of pure holdings. When Christ's birth takes form where will the written Scriptures lead? This will all align to the Word of the Old Testament because it is all true and right.

[11] For the life of a creature is in the blood, and I have given it to you to make atonement for yourselves on the altar; it is the blood that makes atonement for one's life. Leviticus 17:11 NIV

The base of knowing where to align is had in the witness of God not the idea of Him. I know I am tying my heart to His calling, and I have the will to pursue Him in a justified way. Why is there no other more valued than Christ? He is all-encompassed and worthy of being praised. I now am not without the light within me. I have the reward of being one who knows the work of God and how He operates. In His manner, it is developing sharing the ritual of His lead. I aim to Him in favor not loss. Knowing Him garnered to me the plan of a witness in where faith is abundant, and directives are more than losses. I am not the reason one can learn. It is from on high that man finds the way forward. I know there is no other committed to my welfare than the Holy Redeemer. How is this to be? I do not know the answer for it is God alone who knows the plan, but I read the truth and know it speaks to the forward alignment of God to His people. I invite the way to man to find the prosperity to the One of hope not the devil who has no unity of any intent worthwhile. Grow in the way of a saving power and feel the support from God's leading. I realize not all have the idea of sharing the Word but the one who places his heart in the hand of God will have an abundance of knowledge to guide another to Christ. God does not lose His way when it comes to the lighted path of insight. The unity never fades where man has the knowledge of who made him. God works so I too am tying my heart to His counsel. I will align to Him for all time and be given the meaning to a goal that is right. I have the Word to fall back on when I feel lost or without purpose. It does not happen on a regular basis due to my prayer life and the hope it provides. Leading is a simplistic idea where God is the perfect support beam.

My knowing way is due to the Savior's influence not my own. I care for His claim to me and to the man who places value to His person. Leading is not a viewpoint of no offered role of hope. It means to allow another to perform for the better of man not himself. I have an abundance of care to offer, and I will do so with concern not harm. I know the leading of God is for any who place the value of His counsel to their hearts and minds. Would you behave as someone with no appetite for value if you found something of sure standing and cast it aside? No, no one would do such a thing for man desires to offer hope to others with the presence of clear insight unless he is honoring the false god of Satan. His deceptiveness is far and wide one of no hope. He is not one to align to the plan of God for he deems himself above the Almighty! Why would one even begin to think such a thing? I cannot fathom how this takes form, but I realize it happens nonetheless. Many have fallen prey to the idea no other is good enough so why offer hope to any person. Such a manner of insight is false idea making in where no real value is witnessed. I know God can offer the goal of leading and He can venue to man the response of hope with ease. He never loses value or needs another's aid so one can bank on His merit. The need to see Him is not a wise unity either. Faith is in the one where hope is present and leading is called into action. I have the witness of shared unity, so I uphold the role of authoring the insight I have been granted. It came due to study efforts and acceptance of God's moral character. I have the manner of His support, and I tie to Him in unity. I love the witness of His caregiving, and it makes for a good, offered role model to me. I look to another only concerning aid in the physical way. I can spiritually know God speaks to me, so I invest in His support and lead where able. To know the reward of God's care is to align to His support with intent. Giving another the aptitude of a shared biological input is not for all to have claim to. I alone have been given the reward of sharing the birth of the Savior; yet I do not have pride due to it. I work with caregiving not self-ideas. The love value is for me to adhere to God not to turn away from His value.

The God of man is not the way to have life with no purpose. He is the mainstay of man's heart and mind. Where the love of God is favoring all hear Him speak. What matters to the person who places his value in the palm of God is whether the witness he provides is just and sure. The goal of man is to align to the perfect way of Christ. How all this happens is for God to know alone. Man is not the Waymaker he is merely made in the image of God, but this too is not understood completely. I have the desire to align to God with perfect compliance. He is the way to gift my heart to others and to ascertain where to stand in the knowing way of unity. Provide the people with hope and offer the love value of the Savior and you will hear the meaning of the Gospel message. Is this to be heard before the birth of my Child? I do not have the answer to it. I simply believe in the power of God, and I wait for the explanation to be provided. I now realize I am here for the purpose of sharing the honor of carrying the Babe of light. He is the reason I am created. The hope He offers is for every being who places value to Him above all else. I work to offer another work of my hands in where I support the One of insight. Reading the Book of influence is a way to hear the references of God and to know His idea for man to have an abundant life. The glory of a shared unity is not one of no faith. I am here to offer this knowledge in a caring way. Should I ever feel lost or alone I have the Scriptures to lead me into faith where I find the support needed to give hope to mankind. I share this due to the offering of light I witness. The goal of the Word is to offer insight to man, so he better adheres to the God of all. Knowing the fruit of the Word is a gift none compares with. To be knowing where to gift insight comes where man places the knowledge he gains to others in need. It may be a simple gesture of light that portrays the value of love of the King in a unique way. Not all create in the same fashion. We all have different ideas that maintain our hearts and minds with goals of beauty.

The fruit of knowing who the power source is and who is merely penetrating the heart with no support is a favor one needs to recognize. God is not one to offer a false idea in where knowledge is not of an important value. In Him is the sequence of a shared mind. He ordains the heart to enlist with support as He is favoring to mankind. I look at the many who have fallen due to expecting wealth or fame. If you desire this as the only thing of value to you Satan will enter the scene, and you will favor him for it. Be standing on the merit of God and work with the life-giving ability He offers. You will learn the manner of Him and find the faith needed to claim a righteous plan, so others hear the knowledge of Scripture through your actions. God is the Gateway who knows how to align to man. He is a gift in that He performs so man finds support. The all-knowing capital of God is far greater than the work of his people. God carries the heart to the stand of Him so he can operate with pure intent. He can take a misfortune and make it glow with purpose. God is just with clarity, so He is the way to know prosperity. Value of Him feeds the reward and shows the bearer the right plan of action in where faith guides and learning is had. I aim to align to the care of God and find His manner fit to follow. It takes knowing where to learn and what to say to perform for His valued way. Man likes to have his own way where he steps and watches with hope. But know those gifts are not from the Savior. It takes the heart time to evaluate the lead of God and to answer His intent with action. If a dream is glorious but has no footing in the Scripture sense know God is not the one offering it. You must build as God would deem for the ladder of hope to stay in line with the plan of God's witness. I have the work of God, yet I do not always know where it is leading. I invite the Lord to show me where my daily steps are to proceed. I am tying my insight in the perfect way God operates. It means I must wait on His directive to be understood. I have the witness to share the right hope and in the way of it I stand with care. I know where to gift another the value of God but to do so without the aid of God is a false lead. We need to hear the true nature of God's calling. It may be we are to craft on His behalf and never have the success of the offering. This may be difficult for man to realize but God's work is different and not of our own unity. He has the path for us to follow. So, make the Word your stand of insight and you will know the way to offer forward the love of Him, so another has feeding inspired value. The record will be a birth of goal making.

The work of the Savior is mighty and true. He is ever one to perform so man finds abundant light to his call. I have the work of God: yet I do not know how it will take form outside of giving birth to a King. I know I will need to offer growing options of hope for this Child to have the way of God before Him. I agree with this idea, and I offer it already in my prayer support. I aim to verbalize to Him I need His counsel above my own but to teach Him to unite to His own knowledge will be unique. I am not holy nor am I all-knowing. It takes me the same type of understanding process as any other human being to learn or gain knowledge. I now realize it took time to align to God in such a formation that He would use me to guide this hope of mankind. I do not have the offered information for all life to align to Him, but I claim God as the knowledge I learn from. I invite the Scriptures to me, so this offers me a plan and a guidance lean. I value my Lord and He accompanies me in my plan making. We work together so we team with care. I know I can relate to man where the light is prevalent, and the work of my heart builds the reconning of God forward. I value the One who prepared my spirit to match His way. I aim to offer this gift to any who grants me the work of their heart to me in a personal way. I value the team building that transpires and in the flame of recognized hope I am favored. The savoring of a shared hope is not all I have to offer for God has shown me where to gift His counsel. I can gift it to all who ask me how I came to be carrying the Child of prosperity. It takes time to know your intent. Do you place value to the Gateway of hope or are you thinking you have a better math equation to guide you? Man has for generations believed he could master the earth and its rotation. But in truth man has no ability to do this. It means the goal of his support is not the same as God's. I instruct the same care to others who read the Book of light and in doing this witness truth is present. I shall not abide in the valley of death for God has prosperity for those who follow Him in support.

[21] *"Submit to God and be at peace with him; in this way prosperity will come to you. Job 22:21*

The unity of the spirit filled God we have as lead will always guide us with a tender influence until the point of no return. The bypass of a shared idea comes before the heart of one who places his armor in God's light. I now own no property as women here aren't allowed to; yet I am ever sustaining my heart with pure love. I know where to apply the love value and in the way of a shared value from on high I thrive. Growing hope builds. I work to author more faith to those in need. It is a way for me to work with clear intent and not one of confusion. God offers me some intellect in where the love of His counsel is heard. The glory to Him is supportive and I offer it as frequently as I can. I know it can mean I have to adjust my output to that of God's perfect way, so I never offer something other than true gain. I have the work of His support, and this sustains me. I am always being guided to the way of care, so I know I have the heart of His support. He has taken me to Him in such a way I know I am tying others as well. Should I expect a great revenue to happen? He does not promise such an inheritance. Leading is found to be that of a wise idea if hope is the guidance tool. I look at what the abundancy comes from, and I know it is acclaimed by the power of God. The factor of Him is all encompassing and this means I am tied with unity. I exclaim to the world God is right and true, and this means I know Him. He is ever with courage and a lean of intent meeting the man of faith to find love. I value His support more than my own ideas, so I know I am standing with insight. God favors me and this means to be a solid identity in where the support favors my longing. I look to God to evaluate the lead, so I now retain more than a witness of no hope. I am leading so another will find the support I know. Why does it matter to me to do this? God is the plan, and I merely spread the hope of it.

The hope of man is not in his own merit but that of God's viewpoint. In the work of God is the stand of value all need to thrive and lead a life of value. Where the knowing stand is in the corner of God's garment. I have the knowing aptitude He is ever with me so working to share this wealth is all-encompassing. Why do I believe I can relate to others concerning where to find support is due to my own experience in the way of faith. God is my focal point, and I have the accepting value to His way. Sharing is for the man who knows the will of God and who aligns to His manner out of inspiring insight. I work to have the favor from God and in the way of His teaching I find prosperity is abundant. He directs my goal making and I have the Word of God in my spirit. I am tying the honor of God's caregiving to me in a personal way. I shelter in so others find my direct learning for themselves. I have taken the course to study on a regular basis and in the way of sharing it forward others gain with courage how to operate. I look at where the value of Christ is at, and I engage with His person. To pray with clear meaning is to gift my own self with support in where God hears my hope, and He caters to my intent. Do I always know the best thing for my own understanding? Not all is within me to do so. I have the knowledge God is superior to me and He never loses my heart and mind to the negative. Knowing God is a reward I have been gifted. It came when I first accepted Him with free abandonment. I was not old enough to record the event, and I am thankful for the realization God supported me with insight even in the infancy stage. I act with the Word on my heart, so I enter the love of God with hope. He instructs me how to lead and in the goal of His counsel I am fed. Leading is not for the weary or the misinformed. It takes the heart of a person to align to God with purpose. In the honor of God is the plan of a witness that inspires the mind to be present in the way of faith. I am not the lead to man, but the voice of God speaking is within me.

My goal for the people of my region is to know the living God of all. He is ever faithful and true and without blemish. I have the work of His support, and I turn to Him for comfort. Knowing the way to align to His person is to stand on the merit of Him. I look to His support for all I invest toward. I learn how to impart to man the ability I gained in the way of shared, spiritual leading. Grow with unity and tie to the love of the Creator. In Him is the faith one has the will to learn from. I have the gain of sharing the light and in the manner of its glow I tie with hope. To gain in the way of faith is a stand man designs with prayer. Lead with certainty and hear the wise developed Word to know where to contribute and how to offer it to others. I am not the Gateway, nor will I ever be but to know the Creator is a sign of favor. Leading is for all who hope to enlighten and in it is the path of clear knowledge. I now have the work of God to fulfill and the sign of this is my calling. I am to unite in the way I share the hope to my Child. It will be the stand of hope man needs to gain the reflective goal of Him to his heart. Hearing where to stand is to know the gift of support is ever within the heart and mind. I can gain if I apply my intent to God not the enemy of Him. To know the way to contribute so that another has the intellect of caregiving is to ascertain unity and feed it more standing. This takes the sponsor of a shared value in that God must be the reason for the faith to exist. Others may claim God is not the way to thrive, but they have no unity to Him if they process thoughts in this way. I am not the reason to learn Scripture, but I can say I have the support of it in a personal way. This too can be of your intake if you adhere to the way of God and feed your heart His way of being. Shelters are made to be a barrier against the elements of the weather, but they do not keep the enemy at bay. Prayer and reading the Book of Hope are what determines how the mind will operate. The support of a unity in where man ties to the One of hope is a balance needed to align to Him with care and support. It is not a one-sided relationship. A person must determine on their own God is the way ahead. If this does not happen loss ensues, and little invested outward hope is had. The inner side to man must always be a witness to the light. It takes courage to act in the public and to declare God is supportive to you. I have the work of God in me, and this means I am not without hope. He is ever my faithful partner, so I am never alone in my offering. Stand with care and know the Lord is available to live in the way of support. If you are weak with the influence of the world, be united to God and read Scripture to gain support from on high. It feeds the heart, and you will then be more satisfied by the presence of God to you.

Feeding is a goal I have for man to find the hope I know and love. Why would it make a difference to me who learns of God's favor and who simply stands on his own merit? The dream of one having the light within is a unity no one can compare to. I know the work of God is for all to find His way to them. He invites the man who places value to His calling. I have the Word to lead me and to ordain my heart. It has been the plan of my desire to offer this hope forward. In committing a shared unity, I have the balance of a known faith. It is ever before me with support. I now offer this to others in need, and I plan to continue to do so. I have the attire of a shepherd's garment, and I do not say it in a stand of ignorance. It simply binds me to God even more. He is not one to show off His ordinance to me. He is great and beauty unfolds everywhere He is standing. I now realize I too can hear Him within me. It takes the heart an acknowledgement in the true favor of knowing the Scriptures for this to be realized. God is my scalpel, and He shows me where to align to Him with faith. He is the one who offers me my intake in where both His stand and His intent are heard. I have the work of His counsel, and I align to it with care. I should never invite a false entity or look outside of God's support for there is no other more inclined to my welfare or honor. God supports the one who places his goal making in the palm of His outstretched hand. I know He is ever faithful and good without a single blemish to His person. I look at all I witnessed on His account, and I lean on Him with unity. It means I claim Him as my own Savior. Shall I know this Child as I do my Father, the great I AM? Both will be equal to me in faith. I will enter their presence with every prayer I give thus maintaining the connection in a true manner. Glory to God for His gift to me in a personal way!

Glory is the substance God appreciates in where He is the object of its affection. He creates so all will know Him by name. His work to me is tall and forthright. It may not be a physical reward but spiritually it is real and true. Little comparisons can be made for the goal of God is far above that of man's intent. Structured knowledge is ever a plan for my intellect. I worked to read the true Book of Hope and found it favoring to me with compassion. God is perfect and in Him is the unity I need to flourish. Shall I ever lose footing? I do not have the answer to this question, but I do know there is no other thing that is more bountiful or more inviting. God's favor is a solid investment that teaches me the goodness of His way. He is a calling I am drawn toward. It feeds me with care, and I desire more of God each passing moment. He shoulders me with support, and this is the knowledge I gained. The manner of God is for me to offer Him to any who accept my intent as a good way to live. I speak to those who come before me, and I aim to offer the faith to them I witnessed. Shared value comes and hope builds so to offer this good knowledge is an easy idea for me. I look to God for instruction, and I have the work of His counsel to rely on. He is always the Gateway not I. The support of His lead is far greater than the stand of my own ideas. I am not one to align to anything other than God for He is greatness through and through. I will know the difference if a time comes when I do not know how to continue or whether I am merely being led astray. It will not be an offering of light if I have no plan or idea what I need to complete the reward. To know my Savior is to align to Him with hope. If I tread and find no path to work, I will wait on His support to be learned. I aim for the heart of God not my own vested ideas. He claims me as His righteous love so I will act with reverence and stand on His goal making not my own. A lead will develop, and I will then proceed with care at the forefront of my work.

Knowing all the details of every part in play does not happen to me on a professional level. Only God above can know the inner self and how he will attain the knowledge of His person. To evolve with care into the limelight is a plan of strength and support. A quick rise often entails a harm in that man has a difficult time receiving fame without a harm bearing outcome. If you have grown in caregiving and the hope of God is with all you prospered in knowing God has been aligning His own way in you. The support of Christ will happen and in the stand of it love will be had. I now reside in the care of my God and the work of Him is fed to my heart. I act with support, and I believe it matters how I align in caregiving. To stay committed to the One of hope is to inspire man to know God and to say prayers to His support. In the hope of sharing this reward man finds the susceptive way of light given to him. I value the love of God and how He gifts me the unity. To read the Bible and its contents is to achieve where others do not. In the work of a knowing guard, man finds the faith to be a sign he can operate in. I have known the One of inspiring faith and I have been fed the lead of a true hope bearing individual. The basic need of all is to be given the support of life. Only God is the one who can do this. He alone is the vested courage man needs to grow in a solid way. To thrive in a monetary way is not the hope of man. It is a reward for his efforts in the workforce. God is perfect and good. He is ever with courage, and He grants it to the one willing to perform on His behalf. I am not the reason for the plan of hope to be given. I merely align to the way of it for hope to reside within me. I offered the knowing way to those willing to hear and in doing this I am called good. But the truth is no one is good within, not even the one who knows the fruit of God for man has sin nature to his spirit.

Only God is not tainted in this way. Animals are also in need of direct communication from on high. The abundant lead of God is not a simplistic goal but one of true favor. It requires the heart to achieve a goal of building so others also find the prospering way of light.

12 When Jesus spoke again to the people, he said, "I am the light of the world. Whoever follows me will never walk in darkness but will have the light of life." John 8:12 NIV

My sin is not the way to know the intent of my heart, but it shows my care or the lack of it. Man is not the mirage of no intellect. He offers the way to push forth by supportive knowledge being declared. If the fruit is solid and the care a unity to God good comes by way of it. But where there is no option to learn the truth, no hope is provided. Glory is for the One who builds our hearts and minds in the manner of light not dark thoughts. It takes the spirit a realization to learn what matters to God and what does not. If you operate with care but want your own stand to be given you miss the hope of God to you. The care of God is more than a simplistic bounty in the form of a rich pocketbook. Our intake is not the standard, or the inverted idea God is not the Waymaker. He alone cares far more than all others could ever hope to. Even in combining the unity to man comes the deceptiveness of no heart gain where man invests solely for the idea of self. Man is not the bounty but rather the One of hope is this lead. I have the knowledge I am without the whole content of Scripture for it is alive and it builds me when I read it. The practice of knowing who the value stand is and what matters to all is God above not self. God's glory will surround you when you advance in His stand of inspiring leading. He is the Caring Bridge all need to have hope. He never loses the stand of hope and in Him is the goal of prosperity. I value my knowledge, and I enter it to those willing to hear me. Does it matter how I speak to those who come my way. Surely it does for the right framework needs a good basis to be viewed with love and a stand of insight. Broad is the gateway to death, but narrow is the way to Christ. One needs to hear the truth to have the knowing gift of light within him.

Mirrored is my intake from on high. I have the work of God to support me where I lead with care and an influence of good hope. Should I leave this knit idea and offer another with less value just to be heard by the man of no insight? No, compromise means losing the value of your witness. Man can be fooled into thinking he needs to act as the wicked for acceptance to be had. This is a false understanding for it never contributes to man to be an evil lie. God is the way alone not joined to the enemy in His representation. I have the witness to know this is true, so I do not seek out a false goal in hopes of knowing someone in an intimate lead. Hope is not something without a long unity in where the heart is ever faith bearing and good. The love of God is for the one who places his heart in the palm of God's. If ever I were to think I should value something other than the light, I know it is not of God. I have realized sharing the hope in that I study so I gain in the form of favor. God works in me, so I gain and do not find a longing of the unnatural leading from His heart. God has the vested identity in where all who offer the value of God to another have the witness that He is good. To know this is encouraging to others who require the learning just as I have been gifted. Work is not the idea of a shared faith but of intent. If you offer your knowledge to man so he learns where to gift himself a training, you have supportive learning and not of just initial goal making. Man acts as the way ahead when he is merely the footprint not the impression. I now see I have fallen in times past due to not knowing the lighted formula of Christ's teaching. He may be coming to us in the way of the Child I carry; yet He has always been. I do not hear the Word without the accepting of it. Without the connection to it no gain is rewarded. Scripture ties the spirit to it in the way of a goal of hope not of loss. The inherit leading is created by way of a mission statement God is true to His way of speaking. If you hear a voice of reason, you have been given hope from above. The idea I am not all-knowing is a clear identity and a stand of a shared realization only God is this knowledgeable.

God is so good no other has the capability He possesses to be heard with care and the love of hope always present. The Word of the Savior is mighty and true. In the way of a shared hope man is not given a volume of faith until he decides to worship the Great I AM. I have the knowledge this is an example of hope not intent. Sharing the righteous love of the One who mastered leading an inspired unity is to offer Him your valuable heart. To claim Him as your own is to align to Him with support. The unity of God is for man to have within him where God is the support beam needed to believe. I have the acceptance of God within me, and I find it valued above all else. Knowing the relationship hold of a warrior to his leader is to gift forward the hope of the battle to be won not lost. A right and true insight is the suture of God to me. I have the recognized favor of the Most High. In Him is my commitment of faith due to the love I have for His care designed for me. I invite Him to lead, and I walk where I find the faith guiding me. I aim to be a person of honor not loss. The inherit stand of God is far greater than the work of my own hand. I have not found anything more surefooted. I value the way He offers me guiding insight. It is more than I deserve but He feeds me just the same. I look at the hope of God and I offer it to those who asked me where it resides. I know Scripture is the key to learning this support, so I point them to the effects of the reading. My value system is not marred, nor is it without the love of God within it. He atones for the way I operate and in Him is the support necessary to guide and offer a growing height of love. He is ever sure and true so I never have concerns He will offer something of a dark demeaner. I thank the reasoning of Him as that of a gain not an infringement of no hope. I am tabulated to record on behalf of my God and in doing this action more opportunity is given. Thanksgiving is for the one who places his heart in the core being of God. Is there any other gift more precious than the witness of God to His many followers? I now reside in the care of God not the hand of the enemy. I shoulder the reconning and it claims my spirit to Christ. Will this be any different once I birth this Child I carry? No, for God is all light with true gain so there will not be any discord in the way He operates compared to God the Father. The reality of a shared unity is knowing God is far greater than a gift of no value. To learn on behalf of God is to evaluate the light and determine it is what you desire. Darkness must leave if the heart and mind refuse to partake of its offered lie.

God supports the love I have for Him in the way He deems me to offer light to another. In Scripture the way to offer hope is to read it and gain the value of love. I can know where to ascertain the knowledge and in the forgoing way of faith I align to God due to the will of Him adjusting my heart. I have the work of a warrior in me, and this means I align to Him with care. Why would I ever walk outside of Christ for the fact of Him is far greater than my own ability to prosper? I am committed to lead where the door is presented so at times, I have the knowledge of a necessary gift to be shown forth. I have not offered the way to God to any who asked me to step away from the intent I portray. I know there is no point in offering more wealth if they will not hear the Word for themselves. To fight against the One who made you is a false directive negating the vibrant height of God. The value of Him is more than can be recorded. God is the shouldering one needs to give others the promise of the insight found in God's Word. He is ever faithful to the productivity of the need. I have not lost my faith, nor will this happen for I place value to reading the Book of truth. Will I lose my witness where no faith supports it? Not if I lean into God for all my cares as He is the mainframe I need to blossom and thrive with caregiving aptitude. Leadership is abundant and right if God is the focal point. I will inherit the hope of heaven and in the way of it be maintained for all time. The reward is not slim. It is eternal and true. Leadership will be God's directive and hope will be forevermore.

Author Bio

Robin Arne is an artist and writer who joyfully shares the love of the Father through her creative gifts. Living on a remote farm with her supportive husband, she finds inspiration in quiet days devoted to Christ.

Her life and work are centered on her Savior, whose light guides her steps and fills her heart with hope. Immersed in Scripture, Robin draws from God's Word to express faith, grace, and beauty through her writing and clay artistry.

With a vision to open a studio where she shares her art and faith-filled writings, Robin's desire is to glorify God through every piece she creates—a life anchored in divine love and purpose.

Robin Arne is available for interviews, For more information send
inquiries to: info@advbooks.com

Other books by Robin Arne:

God's Manifestation of the Heart   ISBN: 9781597556897
The Hurts Can Be Repaired   ISBN: 9781597557108
Divorce: The Pain God is Able to Heal   ISBN: 9781597557153

RUTH: God's Favor with a Caress of Truth ISBN: 9781597557672
I Am A Scared Witness   ISBN: 9781597558006
ISRAEL: God's Heartbeat to the World   ISBN: 9781597558297

Available at Amazon.com, advbookstore.com
or anywhere books are sold

*A*dvantage
BOOKS

we bring dreams to life™
advbookstore.com

Robin (Rochel) Arne

www.ingramcontent.com/pod-product-compliance
Lightning Source LLC
Chambersburg PA
CBHW052115090426

42741CB00009B/1815